For my Mayor,
Bill Heidemann

With best wishes!

SUPERVISING POLICE EMPLOYEES IN THE TWENTY-FIRST CENTURY

HW Garner
April, 2019

D1451867

ABOUT THE AUTHOR

Gerald W. Garner is chief of the Corinth, Texas Police Department. He recently retired after serving the city of Greeley, Colorado and its population of 105,000 as chief of police for over 12 years.
Chief Garner's nearly 49 years in law enforcement to date spanned
seven departments in three states. He retired at the rank of division
chief after serving the nationally-renowned Lakewood, Colorado Police
Department for 30 years. Perhaps most important, he spent 15 years
as a sergeant where he worked as a Patrol team leader, detective supervisor, crime prevention sergeant, communications supervisor, public
information officer, watch commander, and crisis negotiator for
SWAT. At Lakewood he worked in virtually every mid- and top-level
leadership assignment it is possible to experience in municipal law
enforcement.

Chief Garner holds a master's degree in Administration of Justice.
He writes and instructs widely on law enforcement leadership topics
and has lectured for the International Association of Chiefs of Police
and the FBI National Academy at Quantico, Virginia. He has
authored 11 other books and over 200 magazine articles on law
enforcement subjects.

SUPERVISING POLICE EMPLOYEES IN THE TWENTY-FIRST CENTURY

A Problem-Solving Manual for Law Enforcement Leaders

By

GERALD W. GARNER

CHARLES C THOMAS · PUBLISHER · LTD.

Springfield · Illinois · U.S.A.

Published and Distributed Throughout the World by

CHARLES C THOMAS • PUBLISHER, LTD.
2600 South First Street
Springfield, Illinois 62704

© 2019 by CHARLES C THOMAS • PUBLISHER, LTD.

ISBN 978-0-398-09275-7 (paper)
ISBN 978-0-398-09276-4 (ebook)

Library of Congress Catalog Card Number: 2019009268 (paper)
2019009268 (ebook)

With THOMAS BOOKS careful attention is given to all details of manufacturing and design. It is the Publisher's desire to present books that are satisfactory as to their physical qualities and artistic possibilities and appropriate for their particular use. THOMAS BOOKS will be true to those laws of quality that assure a good name and good will.

Printed in the United States of America
MM-C-1

Library of Congress Cataloging-in-Publication Data

Names: Garner, Gerald W., author.
Title: Supervising police employees in the twenty-first century : a
  problem-solving manual for law enforcement leaders / by Gerald W. Garner.
Description: Springfield, Illinois : Charles C Thomas, Publisher, Ltd.,
  [2019] | Includes index.
Identifiers: LCCN 2019009268 (print) | LCCN 2019006848 (ebook) | ISBN
  9780398092757 (paper) | ISBN 9780398092764 (ebook)
Subjects: LCSH: Police--Supervision of. | Police administration.
Classification: LCC HV7936.S8 G375 2019 (ebook) | LCC HV7936.S8 (print) |
  DDC 363.2/2--dc23
LC record available at https://lccn.loc.gov/2019009268

For
Law Enforcement's First-Line Leaders of Today
Who Will Become
Law Enforcement's Chiefs and Sheriffs of Tomorrow

PREFACE

Leading first-line law enforcement officers is one of the most rewarding tasks in all of policing. It is also one of the toughest.

Whether you are an acting supervisor, corporal, sergeant, or some other variety of first-line leader, you are absolutely key to the success of your law enforcement organization. As every intelligent chief or sheriff knows, he can jump up and down and shout until his face turns purple and it won't matter a whit unless the first-line leader converts those directions, desires, and concerns into action by the cops in the trenches. Likewise, the officers at the pointed end of the stick probably realize that their complaints, concerns, and questions are unlikely to be answered without the assistance of the first-line boss. To repeat: the law enforcement supervisor is vital to the effectiveness, efficiency, and success of the agency employing him or her.

The purpose of this book is to provide the first-line leader with the tools he needs to excel in successfully handling all of his important duties. Short on theory and long on practical advice, it is intended as a "how to" handbook for the primary supervisor. Situated in the real world of policing as opposed to the theoretical one of the academic, the text contains pragmatic guidelines assembled by a veteran police chief who served for 15 years as a first-line leader.

Chances are, you are already a good leader. This handbook will make you better. It contains the information you will need to succeed as decision-maker, tactician, trainer, counselor, disciplinarian, and officer safety expert. It will help you accurately to evaluate your employees' job performance, serve as an integral part of the leadership team, and lead your people to deliver exceptional customer service. It will, in sum, serve as a true Handbook for leadership success.

As you doubtlessly have figured out for yourself, today's law enforcement employees are by no means identical in personality or work style to their predecessors of even a decade ago. But they are good people with outstanding potential. They, along with their more senior colleagues, are waiting for a great leader to bring out their best. That leader should be you.

G.W.G.

INTRODUCTION

Law enforcement represents one of the most critical, noble undertakings on the face of the planet. It employs some of the most courageous, compassionate people who inhabit that globe. Leading those special people to fulfill their critical roles as both service providers and guardians requires exceptional individuals with exceptional talents. Those individuals are the first-line supervisors of law enforcement.

To carry out their wide array of vital duties those supervisors require a whole toolbox of complex skills. This handbook was created with the purpose of supplying or, where already present, strengthening those skills. Assembled by a veteran police chief who served 15 years as a first-line supervisor, the book provides practical, "how to" advice for confronting and mastering the multiple challenges of the first-line supervisor's life.

Chapter 1 will assist the corporal, sergeant, or equivalent in putting together the varied tools and talents he or she will require to be a successful leader. Chapter 2 delves into what is needed to establish a mutually beneficial relationship between the first-line leader and a group of subordinate law enforcement personnel. Chapter 3 covers the ins and outs of forging a positive relationship with the supervisor's own boss.

Chapter 4 provides backup for the first-line leader faced with making the really tough decisions, while Chapter 5 lends guidance for applying those decision-making skills to tactical situations and critical incidents. Meanwhile, Chapter 6 offers suggestions for competently training police personnel to meet and master all aspects of the contemporary law enforcement officer's incredibly difficult job.

Chapter 7 is designed to help the police boss address one of law enforcement's biggest challenges: preparing officers to produce well-written, informative reports. Chapter 8 will assist the leader in evaluating his or her peoples' mastery of this skill and many others. Preparing accurate, impartial, and meaningful employee performance reviews is one the supervisor's most important duties. This section of the book will help him or her do it well. Then, Chapter 9 will assist the first-line leader with the most vital task of all: keeping his or her officers safe on the street.

The supervisor's sensitive role as employee counselor and confidant is explored in Chapter 10. Next, the first-line boss's obligations as disciplinarian and troubleshooter of employee performance issues are examined in depth in Chapter 11. The following chapter proffers pragmatic advice for dealing effectively yet compassionately with the "difficult" employee.

Chapter 13 furnishes recommendations for responding effectively and empathetically to the citizen with a grievance about a law enforcement policy, practice, or employee. Chapter 14 is devoted to helping police personnel best serve some of those same citizens. The chapter includes time-proven advice for leading team members to provide exceptional customer service for those paying the freight: the tax-paying public. Chapter 15 delivers "how to" guidance for the supervisor who has news media relations duties thrust upon him or her at or following a critical incident or similar newsworthy event.

The handbook's final two chapters strive to give the career-minded leader the skills he or she will need to survive and prosper in the law enforcement organization. Chapter 16 goes into the commonsense talents required safely to navigate the politics and intrigue to be found in virtually very law enforcement or other organization. Chapter 17 will assist the first-line leader in bringing it all together to be the absolute best he or she can be. This final chapter takes a look at leadership's ethics, the supervisor's role as a member of the leadership team, and how to get even better and stronger for the future.

This handbook will equip today's capable first-line leader to excel in his or her vital role of influencing the future of policing. Surely nothing is more vital to an increasingly complex and too-often-troubled society.

CONTENTS

Page

Preface vii
Introduction ix

Chapter

1. **The Toolbox of a Great Leader** 3
   What Do You Need to Know? 3
   What Do You Need to Do? 5
   The Value of a Positive Role Model 7
   There's No Substitute for Courage 9
   Summary 12

2. **Your Relationship with Your Crew** 13
   What They Want from You 13
   What You Want from Them 15
   Assessing Your People 17
   Building a Great Team 18
   Summary 20

3. **Your Relationship with Your Boss** 21
   What Your Boss Expects 21
   All Kinds of Bosses 24
   Working for a Difficult Boss 27
   The Relationship You Both Want and Need 30
   Summary 32

4. **Making the Tough Calls** 34
   The Enemies of Sound Decision-Making 34
   The Elements of a Good Decision 37
   When You Don't Know What to Do 40

Learning by Experience 42
Summary 43

5. **Tactical Decision-Making** 45
   Analyzing the Problem 45
   Basic Principles of Problem-Solving 49
   When Things Go Wrong 52
   Learning from Others 53
   Summary 55

6. **Your Responsibilities as a Trainer** 56
   What Should You Cover? 57
   How to Use a Lesson Plan 60
   Overcoming Training Challenges 63
   Measuring Success 65
   Summary 66

7. **Curing the Report-Writing Blues** 67
   Why Can't They Write? 67
   What Is a Good Police Report? 69
   How Can You Help Them? 71
   Summary 73

8. **Evaluating Employee Performance** 75
   Why Do It? 76
   Traps to Avoid 78
   How to Do It Well 80
   The Follow-Up 88
   Summary 89

9. **Your Responsibilities for Officer Safety and Risk**
   Management 91
   Where Lies the Danger? 92
   Inspecting for Safety 97
   Making Your People Safer 98
   The Value of Role Modeling 102
   Advocating for Safety 103
   Summary 104

10. **Your Role as Counselor and Confidant** 106
    Spotting a Problem 107
    Some Problem-Solving Techniques 111
    You Don't Have to Go It Alone 115
    What Is Success? 116
    Summary 117

11. **Your Obligation as Disciplinarian** 119
    Why Discipline at All? 120
    Doing It the Right Way 121
    The Results You Are Seeking 126
    Summary 127

12. **The "Difficult" Employee** 129
    Unique People, Unique Challenges 130
    What You Can and Can't Do 134
    The Goal You Both Seek 138
    Summary 139

13. **Responding to the Unhappy Citizen** 141
    Hearing Him Out 142
    What Are the Hot Buttons? 144
    Resolving the Issue 148
    Summary 149

14. **Leading Your People to Exceptional Customer Service** 151
    What Your Citizen-Customers Want 153
    Avoiding the Customer Service Pitfalls .154
    Doing It the Right Way 156
    Summary 157

15. **Becoming Mr. Microphone: Handling the Media**
    Successfully 159
    Your News Media Duties On-Scene 161
    Your Personal Media Guidelines 165
    Delivering a Great Interview 168
    Preparing a News Release 173
    Summary 177

16. **Surviving Your Organization** 179
     Taking Care of Yourself 180
     Navigating the Political Mine Fields 183
     The Golden Rule 185
     Summary 190

17. **Pulling It All Together** 192
     The Ethics of Your Job 193
     Your Role as a Member of the Leadership Team 194
     How Can You Get Even Better? 196
     What's Next? 199
     Summary 202

Index 205

SUPERVISING POLICE EMPLOYEES IN THE TWENTY-FIRST CENTURY

Chapter 1

THE TOOLBOX OF A GREAT LEADER

Throughout your law enforcement career you have been assembling the tools that have made you a skilled investigator, a compassionate and competent cop. You have accumulated those skills, abilities, and knowledge from many different sources, not the least important of which has been experience. All of those things taken together have helped to make you the highly effective law enforcement officer that you are.

An effective leader needs a well-stocked tool chest, too. As a leader of law enforcement employees you will need every useful tool you can get your hands on and your mind around as you go about your duties of guiding and directing the efforts of others. There are plenty of things you will need to know. There are things you will need to do. You will find, in the unlikely event that you didn't already know it, that there is no greater or more valuable tool than personal courage. It will mesh nicely with your ability to serve as an exceptional role model for your people.

The process of assembling or adding to your leadership tool box begins with determining just what it is you need to know.

WHAT DO YOU NEED TO KNOW?

You cannot hope effectively and successfully to lead others unless you have first mastered some basic leadership skills. Some of these you may have picked up from life experience. Others may revolve around one of the most basic but powerful tools of all: plain common sense. Yet others you may have collected in the "welcome to supervision" classes your employer has sent you to as a new or prospective supervisor. Still more you may have absorbed through your exposure to books, articles, and Internet content on the complex subject of leadership. Finally, you may have obtained even more practical assistance via wide-ranging conversations with successful, veteran supervisors.

It is just fine to assume that you already know a lot about what you are doing and how you are doing it. Self-confidence is a necessary trait for a good leader, too. But hopefully your store of knowledge includes one fact that every exceptional leader has learned by hard experience: you have never learned all there is to know. There is always more to grasp that will make you an even better, stronger leader. The journey to becoming a truly great leader is a never-ending one.

Every leader's book of knowledge, skills, and abilities reads at least a little differently than that of every other leader. There should, however, be a common core that every good leader shares. These people value such cardinal rules of leadership as:

- Praise in public; correct in private.
- Always tell the truth.
- Keep your promises.
- Demonstrate fairness and impartiality in all your actions.
- Strive to serve always as an exceptional role model for your people.
- Always give your best and expect the same of others.
- Be ethical always; follow the rules and don't cheat.
- Demonstrate loyalty to your peers, your subordinates, your superiors, and your organization.

Obviously, many more attributes of a great supervisor could be added to a list that would go on for pages. But you get the idea. Fill your toolbox with proven leadership skills. Then, learn how to use them well.

You should have a good grasp of the technical aspects of your job as well as your organization's policies, procedures, orders, and regulations. How do you check reports by computer terminal? What are the guidelines for taking a citizen's complaint on an officer? What needs to be done following an injury accident involving a police vehicle? And so on.

You likewise need to be knowledgeable about the life stories that are your employees, at least to the extent that you reasonably can know them. Who are they? What do you know about their families, their history, their aspirations? Your agency's records can tell you some of this. Search them out. Talking with your people can tell you a lot more. You can learn much about what happened before you entered the picture. In other words, what does their past look like, good, bad, and otherwise? You need to know in order to do the best job of leading them.

By talking with your employees you can learn about their goals, desires, strengths, and challenges. By listening attentively you also can find out what your people want from you, their supervisor. That is an especially valuable piece of information to have.

Your leader's toolbox also should include a basic knowledge of human psychology. What makes people tick? How can they be motivated to excel? What miscues must you avoid in your efforts to lead them?

You should know as much as possible about the environment you all work in. What are the special challenges facing your organization or law enforcement in general just now? What guidance or directives have you received from your own supervisors? Where do you and your subordinates fit into the larger picture that is the law enforcement agency and the surrounding community of public safety consumers? All of these things and much more you need to know in order to be a truly effective leader. Ask questions. Seek answers wherever you can find them.

WHAT DO YOU NEED TO DO?

Once you have learned where it is you all are expected to go and what it is that you are expected to accomplish, you want and need for your people to follow you there. It is no longer enough to say simply "go do good police work." Life and the society you labor in are way too complicated today for general instructions to have great value. Your people will want to know the goals and objectives that you want them to meet. Most will want to see the bigger picture. They want to know where you are leading them. To gain their trust enough for them to want to follow you there, you must do several things, and do them well. Things such as:

Set the standards. You are the positive role model your employees need to see and hear. You cannot afford to let them down. You must set a great example.

Set and disseminate clearly the goals of the work group. This is the road map that you want your people to follow. But to do that they need to know what it says. Make your expectations as clear as you possibly can.

Keep the lines of communication open. It is the surest way to keep your team on task, clear on what it is they are supposed to be doing and how they are supposed to be doing it. Ask and welcome questions to be sure everyone understands expectations.

Establish personal connections. Some call it empathy or just plain caring. People are willing to do more and better work for someone they believe actually cares about their well-being. That someone should be you.

Be both fair and consistent. Your team members want to know what to expect from you. On the other hand, their own expectations of you include consistency and impartiality in the way you treat them. As you know, police employees can be a super-critical audience. Do not disappoint them.

Be truthful and honest with your subordinates. Unless they can have faith in your absolute credibility they will not trust you, with all the accompanying negative fallout that radiates from that lack of trust. Tell the truth even when you know the message will not be well received.

Represent their interests. Your people will expect you to go to bat for them when necessary. They want to know that you are in their corner, even when things are not peachy and they may have disappointed you. Representing them does not mean shielding them from earned consequences.

Display technical competency. Your officers won't expect you to be the best cop on the street or in the detective bureau. They *will* expect you to have a cop's sense and be able to do the basics of a cop's job if called upon.

Show loyalty in all directions. That means up, down, and sideways. You must support the agency's top leadership staff, your fellow supervisors, and your employees in every way in which it is ethical and lawful to do so.

Display vision. Share the bigger picture with your followers, not just what is expected of them today. Emphasize their role in the vision you and the organization's leaders are seeking. Recognize that they are intelligent people and can grasp it.

Exercise your common sense. Your subordinates will expect you to have it in spades. It will help you solve a problem for which no specific policies or guidelines exist. Common sense is the sum of life experience, native intelligence, and a "feel" for the situation at hand. Do not hesitate to apply it.

Be known for reliability. Your employees must have faith that when you say you are going to do something for them it is guaranteed to be done. A reliable leader keeps his word no matter what. If for some reason you cannot make good on a pledge you owe your people an explanation as to why.

At the same time, there are some broken tools that should never be found in your bag. Frequent displays of temper towards your subordinates should not happen. Yelling or cursing at your people is never acceptable, no matter how great the provocation. Playing favorites and showing partiality towards one or more of your employees is also unacceptable, as is holding a grudge and seeking the opportunity to "get even" with a subordinate. Distorting the truth through intentional omissions or outright falsehoods is likewise forbidden to the ethical law enforcement leader. Your believability must mean everything to you. Failing to show loyalty to anyone or anything is absolutely denied an honorable leader, as well. Finally, setting a poor example in anything is never acceptable behavior from a leader of your caliber. It cannot be allowed to happen.

Defective tools can cause a lot of damage. They even can be dangerous. See to it that your toolbox never contains any.

THE VALUE OF A POSITIVE ROLE MODEL

You are an exceptional leader. Or you will be one after just a little more work. Your goal is to have your employees want to be like you. That probably would be the highest compliment they could give you. You do what you expect to see them doing. You say what it is you want them to say. You act like you want them to act. And you do all of it consistently. There is no "day off" from being a great role model.

Your morale is catching, so you want your team members to see you at your positive best. But you are also a realist. You don't expect the sky to rain honey when the outhouse blows up. All the same, you do not damn your organization or its leadership in front of your troops. To your employees and the public your organization and its people are always top notch. By the same token, you never display your fears and doubts in the presence of your personnel. They want to know that their leader is both compassionate and unafraid. Their leader is you. They need to view their leader as a good cop and a solid, courageous boss.

Since you expect your officers to look good, you must set a positive example for them. That requires that you always appear well-groomed and properly attired for the job. If your role is a traditionally-uniformed one, your leather or composite gear always look bright and clean. If you work in a soft uniform or in plain clothes, you dress appropriately and never look like you slept in your garments or just climbed out from under the car after changing the oil. Your level of fitness is important, too, if you want your troops to emulate you. The same holds true for the language you use around your subordinates. If your words are sometimes a bit too salty for polite company, you should not be surprised if your troops sound like sailors, too.

Readily admit your mistakes when you make them, as being human you certainly will. Your people expect you to be a role model, but they also know you are human. They don't expect perfection, just a human being that they can admire and follow. Admitting your errors actually helps to build your credibility. Fix the mistakes whenever you can and apologize when necessary.

Do not be overly concerned with quickly "fitting in" with a new work team. Be yourself. It will be plenty good and most people will accept you for what you are, not what you may be pretending to be.

Don't lower your expectations of your subordinates if they do not adhere to the same high standards that you do. Whether it is in job skills or ethical practices or something else, you want to bring your team members up to your standards if theirs happen to be lower than your own. Your team members (or most of them) are better than that. Do not disrespect them by expecting less than their best. Your personal goal should be to strive constantly to get better at what you do. It is not unreasonable to expect the same of your people.

Serving as an excellent role model includes treating everyone—employee and citizen-customer alike—with courtesy, respect, and impartiality. It includes consistently displaying real loyalty, too. Loyalty to your employees, your organization, and the community you all serve. But there is something more. . . .

THERE'S NO SUBSTITUTE FOR COURAGE

It is almost a given that a law enforcement leader must possess and demonstrate personal courage. If the would-be leader expects his charges to be willing to search a darkened structure for a dangerous offender, he certainly must be willing to do the same. His people will expect it. If he is truly a leader, he will expect it of himself. You will, too.

A word of caution, however. It is perfectly understandable that a supervisor, particularly one who is new in the role, would want to show his or her bravery to subordinates. At the same time, on occasion the supervisor's proper place is directing the operation, not personally participating in it. For example, a supervisor who is preoccupied with performing safely in a hide and seek search for an offender may not be able to distance himself sufficiently from the ongoing tactical events to grasp the overall situation and think clearly about what is to be done next—and how. In one real-life incident, a new sergeant experienced the tragedy of having one of her officers killed during a search in which she was personally participating. The criticism later directed at her was that she should have directed the operation, not taken part in it as one more searcher. Entirely fair or not, the criticism became something she would have to live with for the remainder of her life.

Sometimes a supervisor, particularly a new one, will overdo it in the displayed courage department in order to impress his or her officers. That practice can result in foolish, risky, unnecessary chances being taken. It is often termed Tombstone Courage, and it's the last thing a police officer needs to see displayed by his leader. Bad things, including the spilling of blue blood, too often flow from such foolhardy displays.

There are other ways besides making foolish tactical decisions in which you can demonstrate the absence of true courage. Some of them reveal the absence of what is sometimes called administrative courage, as opposed to the physical variety. Administrative courage requires that you do the right thing even when it is not the easiest thing, even when it may not be popular with others. People who "go along to get along," even when they know the chosen path is the wrong one, often lack administrative courage.

Critical mistakes in which a leader can demonstrate a lack of courage of any kind include the following examples:

- A supervisor fails to back a subordinate whom he knows has done the right thing.
- A supervisor blames a peer or superior for an unpopular decision that he actually authored himself.
- A supervisor commits an act he knows to be easy but unethical.
- A supervisor tells a lie to get out of a tight spot he created for himself by his poor performance.

Loyalty is a component of real courage, too. Loyalty to peers, subordinates, superiors, the community, and the organization he or she is a part of, that is. Integrity is a part of genuine concern, too. Cheaters and dishonest people inevitably lack true courage. They are more interested in doing the easy thing than the right one.

Courageous leaders also are consistent in their decision-making and in the corrective actions they take involving their employees. Their subordinates do not have to worry about whether they are dealing today with Darth Vader or Luke Skywalker, a tyrant or a fair boss. To be reasonably content, employees need to know what to expect from their supervisor in good times or in bad. For your troops, that boss is you.

Your employees will expect you, their trusted leader, to display courage even when those around you are doing anything but. Sometimes this is termed self-control. Competent, admired supervisors are expected to have it in ample supply. Demonstrating courage and self-control when all those around you have misplaced theirs will make you stand out—in a good way. Your people want to see that. They need to see it.

The courageous supervisor—that's you—should not be preoccupied with what is popular or trending today. He does not need to be schooled on the latest pop management buzz words. He or she must instead concentrate on saying and doing *what's right*. As a courageous leader your ethics and sense of fair play are never for sale, not at any price.

Personal courage enables you to face the dangerous, armed felon. Administrative courage causes you to make the unpopular decision because it is the right thing to do. Personal and administrative courage are elements of something else that every ethical and effective leader must possess. It is called *command presence*. Simply put, it means I am here, I am competent, I am in charge, and everyone should know it. It evidences self-confidence that does not stray into arrogance. You cannot lead men and women of today's law enforcement workforce without it. Courage is a necessary component of command presence.

You must never cease adding tools to your leader's toolbox over a long and contributing leadership career. If you are truly wise, every day and every experience will hold the promise of learning something new, something that will make you better. Seek those moments. Be receptive to what they can teach you. Be willing to accept something that may fly in the face of something else you knew, or thought you knew. Never close your mind to new knowledge.

As life experience already may have taught you, learning can at times be found in the most unexpected places. Some of the very best leaders have developed their leadership style (or toolbox) from studying the mistakes of others, including other leaders. Failure, it seems, can be an exquisite teacher. Don't overlook its opportunities for learning. Benefit from others' miscues and misfortunes.

Finally, leave sufficient room in your tool box for a big supply of common sense. Made up largely from life experience and your own, innate intelligence, common sense will aid you greatly in your decision-making endeavors. If you'll just listen, that quiet little voice in your head may caution you not to proceed with a certain course of action. It may warn you of potential, negative consequences, including unintended ones. You ignore your common sense's little voice at your own peril.

By now your leader's toolbox should contain at least a starter set of tools. The next chapters will add many more very useful ones.

SUMMARY

An effective leader like you needs a lot of reliable tools to do his or her job well. Some of those tools, like honesty, courage, and credibility, are time-honored ones. Their great value has been proven in long use by a lot of great leaders who have gone before you. The utilitarian value of solid common sense belongs in your collection of absolutely necessary tools, as well. Other tools are newer. Technical competency with today's increasingly-complex law enforcement equipment and practices provides an example of one of the newer and still-evolving ones. You are unlikely to be required to be a subject matter expert in exactly how these things work, but basic familiarity with the principles will be expected of you.

You also will find the tools of positive role modeling and excellent communication skills to be absolutely necessary for the successful leader. Add to them sincere empathy and a genuine interest in your people and you will have a particularly valuable set of tools for leading a team of law enforcement employees. An earned reputation for trust, reliability, vision, and loyalty will be no less valuable to you as an effective tool for an exceptional supervisor.

By now your leader's toolbox already includes a collection of the proven-dependable tools that will make you a highly-competent supervisor and an exceptional leader. Promise yourself to keep adding to that collection throughout your leadership career. It will serve you well as an outstanding leader of law enforcement personnel.

Chapter 2

YOUR RELATIONSHIP WITH YOUR CREW

A leader's effectiveness, or lack of same, is largely dependent upon his or her relationship with others. It really is as simple as that. If you have trouble getting along with other people, you will have even more trouble leading men and women in law enforcement. It is a fact of life that normal human beings tend to work harder and better for someone that they truly like and respect. None of this means that you have to try and ingratiate yourself with your employees by failing to do your job as their boss. It doesn't mean you have to organize a fun picnic at lunch daily. All you have to do is your job—the right way. That means serving as the active, involved, communicative leader that you are.

You crew is your "other family." In the work world of law enforcement, you may find that you spend as much time (or more) with your work family as you do with your loved ones away from the job. That reality does not require that you have to love your employees like your children. But the reasonable amount of good will and good feelings that can develop between a good and fair boss and his or her subordinates is a natural and positive thing. It's a relationship you are seeking as an effective leader.

WHAT THEY WANT FROM YOU

Working with a team of law enforcement personnel, sworn or non-sworn, is just that: a team effort. Each of you depends upon the other members of the group to share equally the burden and the risk. As the group's formal leader, your load is the heaviest of all. You are expected not only to do your own work and manage your own risks but guide a group of other people in safely and successfully handling theirs. It is what you signed up for when you accepted the title of supervisor.

Cops and their kin expect a lot from those who would profess to lead them, especially in a field assignment. As the boss, your officers will expect you to be consistently honest, open, and forthright with them. They will want the unvarnished truth from you, even if you all know that what they hear is not going to please them. You expect the absolute truth from them. It is not out of line for them to expect the same from you in return.

Your people want to know that you will have their back when "stuff" happens. They do not have a right to expect you to lie for them or shield them from the just consequences of any bad behavior. But they *can* expect you to give them a break when you can and energetically defend them against unfair treatment from above. They want to have the benefit of the doubt and your unflinching trust once it has been duly earned. Once they have justified your trust they will count on you to believe them when their word contrasts with that of an evil-doer.

Your people want to be heard out in any controversy or conflict. They want to be able to present their side of events without interruption. They want to be given the opportunity to *explain,* even if you do not ultimately agree with their explanation.

Your officers desire that you know them by name, as something more than a body that can fill a beat or a desk chair. They want you to know something about them, even if it is only that they have two kids and a wife named Liz. Once more, this is not an unreasonable expectation. It would not be unreasonable for you to expect the same from your own boss.

Naturally, your subordinates want you to treat them fairly. They want that decency and impartiality to extend to all facets of their work relationship with you. Beyond that, they want to be kept in the know about what is going on organizationally. The rumor mill flourishes where accurate information is lacking. Police officers may be without peer when it comes to creating and passing rumors. By keeping your people accurately informed to the maximum extent permitted by your own boss's restrictions you make the ground where rumors take root and grow less fertile.

Your support for your officers' interests in the areas of safety and survival is a top priority. Your cops need to know that you are always out front seeking the best available officer safety policies, procedures, equipment, and training for them. The troops likewise need to know that when they did it the right way in the interest of officer safety yet someone outside or inside the organization squawks about it you will be there to defend them. Failing to do that will cancel out virtually anything else you have done to earn your officers' support.

Your personnel expect to be recognized for good work. Even if you cannot give them a monetary reward or a plaque for the wall, they will want to know that you acknowledge the exceptional job they have done. They may be willing to settle for an "attaboy" or "attagirl" from the sarge (which can, by the way, be a very powerful motivator), but they will expect some kind of deserved recognition.

All of these expectations can be summed up thusly: your employees desire and expect your *loyalty* as their leader. It's no more than you expect from them. The expectation quite reasonably extends both ways. Loyalty requires truthfulness, honesty, openness, and personal courage all around. It calls for everyone doing his or her best and sharing equitably in the work and the potential hazards. When viewed in this light loyalty can trump every other legitimate expectation that your people can demand of you.

There is one more thing that really good (and courageous) leaders do for their followers. They ask of their charges what they can do to help them in their jobs and careers. Maybe one of your employees is seeking a good but expensive specialized training class. Maybe another wants you to help her get better at report writing. Perhaps another wants you to loosen up just a little on the supervisory leash that he perceives. Whatever the case, you won't know their desires unless you ask and listen attentively to what you hear. Unlike Aladdin, it's unlikely that you can or should grant every wish. It can nonetheless prove helpful to have the conversation. It is one more way of showing that you really do care. But be sincere. Cops are by necessity very good at sniffing out fakes. Be sure you actually feel the interest and empathy you are showing.

WHAT YOU WANT FROM THEM

Put directly, you want from your team members many of the very same things they want from you, their boss. For starters, your reasonable expectations should include the following:

Truthfulness. Lying by omission is still lying. So is telling only partial truths. You have the right to expect that your team members will tell you the truth in all things, big and little.

Integrity. It's tied closely to truthfulness. Expect your employees to demonstrate honesty and openness in all of their dealings within and without the law enforcement organization.

Their best. They want it from you; you must have it from them. A law enforcement officer's ethics demand it. The organization and your citizen-customers have a right to expect it, too.

Courage. It amounts to more than going after an armed criminal, as important as that is. You should expect personal courage from each member of your team. That includes the willingness to make the right and ethical decision when it feels easier to do something else.

Trust. In their supervisor's motives, that is. Until and unless you prove otherwise, and hopefully that will never happen, your employees should assume that the decisions you make and the actions you take have their best interests at heart. Assuming you are an honest and ethical leader, that is not an unreasonable expectation for you to have of your people. An organization or work group lacking mutual trust is destined for failure.

Loyalty. Yes, you have read or heard that word often. But there is a good reason for the repetition. Loyalty is that important in the law enforcement profession. You must hold your people accountable to demonstrate ethical loyalty to their peers, their supervisor, and their organization. Ethical loyalty does not allow for lying or cheating to support anyone or anything, however.

Willingness to get better. This one accompanies your expectation that they do their best. You strive to become a better person and a better leader every day, every shift you work. You have internalized that personal goal. It is a part of who you are. You should require the same devotion to personal improvement from each of your team members. Let them know it.

There is nothing unreasonable in any of these expectations. You can and should hold each of them for each of your police employees. They should have them of themselves. (Granted, you cannot mandate that one.) It's how a good team and a good organization get even stronger.

ASSESSING YOUR PEOPLE

If you are to do your job well, you need to know what you have to do it with. The most valuable commodity you have to do it with are your talented employees. But how talented, how skilled are those employees? They may be the best in the organization, the state, the nation. Or not. But you are not going to know of their competencies, strengths, and challenges unless you make diligent inquiry. You have to have as much information as possible before you can determine what your people are capable of and where they may need some help. It is your job to pull together that vital information.

You will have to do some research. One valuable source to draw upon is the documentation that exists in your agency's records. The data concerning backgrounds, accomplishments, and history will exist in everything from past performance reviews to disciplinary records. Training files and records of commendations and awards should be helpful, as well.

Your supervisory peers may be able to provide a wealth of information. Unless they are brand new hires, members of your crew likely have worked for some of these people in the past. These prior bosses should be able to tell you a lot. You can learn much about special skills and talents as well as potential problems.

Examining your employees' job skills, with emphasis on their written work product, can tell you a lot, as well. Are they good report writers or are they going to need some help? How about basic investigative and interviewing skills? Some of these things you only will learn by observing your people in action. You do not want to appear to be hovering, but you do want to check by and check up. It can come under the guise of "I was close by so I thought I'd see if you needed anything." You desire to leave the accurate impression of an interested boss, not an inspector or micromanager. At the same time, you never can afford to cease observing and thereby learning more about your people. You'll be a more knowledgeable and thereby more effective supervisor for it.

Perhaps the best means for learning about your team members and their abilities is simply to spend time with them in an informal workplace setting. Such sessions might occur over a shared meal or just a cup of coffee. By hearing about what they have done and what they want to do ("I'm interested in promotion.") you can learn a great deal. Strengths, weaknesses, hopes, concerns, fears, and personal goals can present themselves to a good listener. After all, every good supervisor knows that he or she can learn a lot more by listening than by dominating the conversation. They realize that a "good conversationalist" is someone who shuts up and lets me talk about my favorite subject: me.

It is perfectly alright to ask your folks what they would like to accomplish with their life and their career. Don't be surprised if they are surprised by the question. It may be something they have never been asked before. But the query is a valid one, and its answer can tell you a lot. Do not push for a prompt response. It may take some mental processing time for your conversation partner to come up with a thoughtful answer. If you keep the open communication going, however, you are likely to pick up a lot, sooner or later.

Like so much else you do, assessing your people is a never-ending task. The makeup of the work group likely will change periodically. Individual members of the team may change somewhat at various stages of their lives. In addition, the world in which you all labor is constantly changing. For example, requirements for officer legal training will change as the high courts of the land change their collective minds on certain issues. What was a legal and effective law enforcement practice yesterday may not be tomorrow. By continuously assessing your team's performance in the legal environment you could well detect a need for a revision in procedures and practices. Your surveillance and assessment responsibilities are never really at an end.

BUILDING A GREAT TEAM

You can do it. Yes, you will require the active participation and support of your team members. But you, the leader, are the key element in making it happen. You are the nucleus around which a great team can coalesce.

In a perfect world an outstanding team has 100% participation from each of its members. No matter how good a supervisor you are, you may never gain that degree of total support. That's not your fault. You probably did not get to choose your team members. (It's a huge gift if you did!) Do not blame yourself if you have one or more soreheads on the team who choose not to get with the program. More later on dealing with them. But you do need to get as close to unanimous as you can in team support for what you are trying to accomplish. You need it to succeed to the degree you desire.

And just what is it that you are seeking to accomplish? An exceptional team knows the mission and shares in the drive to accomplish it. As the formal leader you will be expected to set and explain that mission and its attendant goals and objectives. Your agency may have helped you with the task by setting some for you. But nothing says you cannot add more of your own. That's what a good leader does. You may elect to have your team members participate in the goal-setting. It is an established fact that oftentimes employees work harder towards reaching goals that they have helped set. Bring your people into your planning process whenever you can.

Good communication among all of the team members as well as between the members and their boss (you!) is another hallmark of a great team. Missions and goals cannot be carried out unless the team knows what they are and why they are a good idea. That burden of clear communication is on you, the team leader. Question your team members about what it is you are all supposed to be doing. Your objective is to find out for sure if each teammate understands his or her directions. Encourage questions from the team. Ask straight out: What questions do you have? What have I missed? What else do you need to know to carry out our mission? Any mission deadlines involved must be made clear to everyone, also.

In the process of discussing ideas and formulating plans it is important that no one's contributions get downplayed or ridiculed. If that happens you probably have received your last contribution from that team member. Real trust only can find a home where every member of the team shows respect for every other member. Trust is a must-have for every great team. As the leader you are the one most responsible for assuring that this sort of atmosphere exists.

These kinds of special relationships are necessary if you are to lead a truly exceptional team. The relationships are strengthened when the leader does not hesitate to offer kudos for a job well done. You must share the commendation with all members of the team who had anything at all to do with the accomplishment. Be sure that the praise is actually deserved based upon what happened. Fake praise does not fool cops. Then, spread the good words around evenly. Recognize, however, that some of your team members may want to receive their praise in private from a leader they admire. Know your people well enough to understand how each prefers to receive praise, public or private, oral or written. Be sure it is awarded in a timely fashion. Praise too long delayed can lose some of its value for the recipient.

Let others know about the good work done by your team. You might consider going through the chain of command to ask for the Big Boss to come to a team meeting and relay some sincere words of praise. A lot of cops deny that such things mean much to them. A lot of those same cops are not being entirely truthful.

Building a great team is a goal of most great leaders. Doing it is certainly within your capabilities as a talented leader yourself. Your team and your organization both will benefit from your earnest efforts.

SUMMARY

You must establish positive relationships with a number of different groups and individuals to be an effective leader. You know that. Of all those none is more important than the members of your team of subordinates, your own work group. Relationships rely on trust and understanding. You help build both by finding out what your team wants and needs from you, their leader. At the same time, you make clear to your team members what you expect from them. It is this mutual understanding that can, over time, build trust.

Assessing and evaluating your crew on a continuing basis will help you in better preparing them for the challenges they will face on the job. In doing that you not only will increase their effectiveness and efficiency, you also will help them to be safer and, for many, boost their overall job satisfaction. You are not personally responsible for their happiness. That is up to each individual. But by doing your part to see that they are treated well you greatly increase the chances that your team members will be loyal, productive guardians of the community. That's not a bad state of affairs for a leader to seek.

Your team members are important to you. That's a given for any true leader. As their supervisor, their role model, you are much more important to them than the chief. You are their close-at-hand boss and they know it. That intimate relationship is the bedrock of a great team.

Chapter 3

YOUR RELATIONSHIP WITH YOUR BOSS

Your team members are very important to you. So are your peers, your organization, and your community. That is as it should be for a good leader. But there is someone else who is very important to you, and that is your own boss. He or she has a great deal to do with your job satisfaction and your career. To at least some extent, your very future rests in your boss's hands. You are by no means selfish or self-absorbed if your relationship with your supervisor concerns you. It should.

Like any successful and mutually rewarding relationship, respect, good communication, trust, and openness are required from each party to the arrangement. That and a whole lot more. You and your boss have both the right and the responsibility to expect certain things of each other. The relationship looks something like this.

WHAT YOUR BOSS EXPECTS

Your supervisor has a job to do and a life to lead. To put it bluntly, he or she is hopeful that you will make both easier and more productive. That hope is not much different from the one you have of your own subordinates. Your boss has a number of expectations of you on the way to making that "hope" a reality. They include the following:

- Demonstrate loyalty. You should not be engaging in back-biting, undermining, rumor-mongering or anything else that could be seen as detrimental to your boss and his or her position. Many bosses view disloyalty as insubordination, a view that will not be helpful to your future with your boss or the organization if he deems you guilty of it.

- Tell the truth. Your supervisor needs to hear the truth and nothing but the truth, even when you know what he hears will anger or disappoint him. He does not want you to color the truth or omit relevant parts of the story. He doesn't want you to delay delivering the bad news, either. Get it in front of him before someone else does. You don't want him to hear some version of the story elsewhere before he learns the facts from you.
- Demonstrate personal accountability. That is especially true when the news is not good and you had a hand in the affair. Never try unfairly to shift the blame to someone else. Your boss expects you to take responsibility for your failures and mistakes as well as your successes and accomplishments. Own your decisions and your actions.
- Be a team player. Yes, it sounds trite. But your supervisor wants you to get along with and support the other members of the leadership team, regardless of whether you like them or not. Big bosses do not like to waste time refereeing disputes among their little bosses.
- Be willing to take calculated risks. Your boss does not want you to be reckless, but neither does he want you to be afraid to innovate and try something new. Progress is made through innovation and a controlled amount of risk. Your boss likely will appreciate the courage you show in sometimes venturing off of the well-trod path. Just don't wander so far that he loses track of you!
- Work to eliminate surprises. Bosses don't like surprises, most especially when the surprise includes bad news. Keep your supervisor well informed. Give him too much information as opposed to too little. He can disregard what doesn't interest him. He will tell you if you are besieging him with too much news or too many details. Your goal is to avoid embarrassing your boss by leaving him out of the know on something his bosses would expect him to know about. It's called the information game and it is played ruthlessly in some organizations. Don't let your boss become a victim of it.
- Handle your team and responsibilities. Your boss has neither the time nor the desire to do your job in addition to his own. As one

law enforcement manager rather directly put it to a subordinate supervisor, "if I have to do your job I don't need you." Rude perhaps, but true. You must not expect your boss to handle tasks you are responsible for. Letting that happen could cause him to suspect that you are lazy, incompetent, or both.

- Assist with the tough tasks. There probably are parts of your job that you do not particularly like. Chances are, your supervisor has some of those, too. Volunteering to handle some of that work for your boss will boost your stock with him or her. Some people do not like to write or do numbers. If you are talented in one of these areas you may be able to score points with your leader by volunteering to take over a task for him. There may be some other areas he could use help in. In the meantime, you are learning his or her job—a career plus for you.
- Follow the exception rule. It means just this: handle the routine stuff so that your boss does not have to get involved with it. Only the out-of-the-ordinary—the exceptional—should require you boss's intervention. It's alright to tell him what you did, just don't ask him *what* to do in routine matters.
- Be reliable. Your boss needs to know that you will do what you say you will do, that your word is your bond. He does not want to have to ding-dong you constantly or ask repeatedly if you have carried out your assignments.
- Bring proof to back up your positions. It is not enough to ask your boss for, say, more troops because your personnel are telling you that you need them. You should be prepared to back up your requests with solid evidence of why you need whatever it is you are requesting. As one Big Boss put it, "I need facts and figures, not your feelings." The statement is brusque but accurate as far as most bosses are concerned. Your opinions based upon your observations and experience are important. But they must be backed up with something tangible whenever possible.
- Don't hand up your boss. It sounds like a given and it is. The temptation may arise from your wanting to ingratiate yourself with your troops or your peers. But joining them in openly criticizing your boss or his policies or his actions will come back to bite you sooner or later. Eventually your boss will learn of your perfidy. When he or she does, nothing good will happen for you. You don't take the risk if you don't engage in the behavior.

None of these boss expectations are unusual or unreasonable ones. You almost certainly have some of the same of your own subordinates. Meeting your supervisor's reasonable expectations will help to build the positive relationship you must have with your boss, no matter what kind of boss he or she is. And speaking of....

ALL KINDS OF BOSSES

There are indeed all shapes, sizes, and varieties of bosses. You likely will have the opportunity to work for several different kinds over your career. And a single boss may fall into more than one category, depending upon the circumstances. Some types include:

The new boss. Because he wants to impress *his* boss by always getting it right, the novice leader is apt to be more than a little nervous about whatever it is you are doing. He may even be insecure in his own mind about his ability to handle his new responsibilities. He may have been doing *your* job only a short while ago. He may ask a lot of questions and seem to lack trust in your competence. The fact is that he just doesn't want you to do something that is going to reflect poorly on him.

Especially if you are an experienced supervisor, the new boss may turn to you for reassurance that he is doing a good job. He may seek your advice often. Let the rookie boss know that you are going to take care of him. Let him know that you are there to help anytime he needs it. Then, be sure you are there when he needs you. As your boss's trust and comfort with you grow, you likely will find that he is backing off at least a bit in his concern that you are doing your work well.

The veteran boss. While it is always risky to generalize, the "old lion" probably will be more secure in himself and his abilities and less likely to haunt your every move. Most likely he will leave the daily operations of your work group up to you, expecting only to be notified of the exceptional event he may need to tell his own boss about.

Treat your veteran boss with the respect his seniority merits. Honor him by asking his opinion or advice from time to time. Let him see that you recognize and honor his experience. But remember that, like any other boss, he expects to be kept apprised of any major happenings involving you and your team members. Even if he *seems* uninterested in what you are doing, you fail to keep him advised at your own peril.

The really nervous boss. He could be a new boss, but he might be a veteran who worries an unusual amount, whatever the reason. He may ask a great many questions and offer a lot of advice. His goal is to look good and stay out of trouble. He is likely to appreciate your helping him do both.

Try to be patient with your nervous boss. Reassure him and patiently answer his questions. Never leave him with the impression that you are in any way irritated with him. With you as his righthand man or woman he hopefully will relax at least a little as he comes to realize you will look out for him.

The hot reactor. He has got a temper and he does not mind displaying it, at least around his subordinates. He may additionally be a bully. He tolerates no argument or disagreement from a subordinate. He may even be a shouter and a curser, to boot. He may think out loud as opposed to processing before talking—or shouting. In sum, he is likely an unpleasant fellow to be around, at least some of the time. Some subordinates have compared working with such a boss to an individual living with a domestic abuser: everyone walks on eggshells, afraid of saying or doing something that will set him off.

Some employees minimize their mental damage brought on by such a boss by minimizing their contact with him or her. That's not an unreasonable strategy, but realistically you are going to have to be around the boss some of the time in order to carry out your own responsibilities. When you do, try your best to maintain your composure even in the presence of repeated provocations. Do not get into arguments with this aggressor. Remain courteous and professional, even if his diatribe appears directed at you personally.

Hard as it may be, do not allow your ego to push you into going head to head with this bully. You are unlikely to win that kind of battle. Respond instead with tact, patience, and calm. Return later, when things have calmed somewhat, to restate your point in a quiet manner. You are not seeking renewed hostility. Some leaders have found good results in sitting down privately with the boss in a quiet moment and telling him how his verbal assaults make them feel. They tell the boss that they know he doesn't mean to hurt, but when he acts that way it really does hurt them. That approach is not guaranteed to work, of course, but sometimes it has. It gives the boss an out—he didn't *realize* he was hurting anyone. It was all accidental. You will have to decide for yourself if it is worth a try with a perpetually angry boss.

There is a good chance that if your boss persists with his childish behavior it eventually will come to the attention of *his* bosses, who do not want hiccups in the organization's smooth operations. They are likely to deal with the boss problem.

The politician/climber. This social butterfly is intent on advancing his career as quickly as possible. There is nothing inherently wrong with that as long as he pays sufficient attention to his responsibilities of the moment. The more extreme version of this species may be quite willing to leave bodies in his wake as he strives to get to the top. You do not want yours to be among them. This is not necessarily an entirely bad boss. He just may be a lot more concerned about his own future than that of his subordinates, including you.

Do your best for this perhaps selfish boss. (You always do.) Keep him in the know even if he comes across as less than interested. You can bet he will become interested and be quick to assign blame if you leave him out of the loop and things go south. If your upwardly-mobile boss does advance and is smart enough to sense your role in his success he may want to take you with him. If you are interested in advancement that's one route to take. You also will have to decide if you want to continue to work with this individual in another assignment.

The incompetent boss. He may be out of his depth in his current assignment. He may not be too smart and the organization missed or ignored that little problem when promoting him. He may be retired on duty and not really into his job anymore. He or she may have major personal issues such as alcoholism or serious marital problems. It could be a combination of these things or something else entirely. Whatever the case, he is not doing his job very well.

It is not your role to shield a bad boss from the consequences of his actions or inactions. Do your best for him as you would for any other boss. Be willing to do some of his work for him if it is needed to keep the ship afloat. Chances are that eventually will come to the attention of upper management. You do not have to trumpet what you are doing beyond your own duties. Do not speak badly of your boss in front of the troops. Have enough faith in your organization to believe that your boss's failings sooner or later will be noted by the Bigger Bosses, who want things to go well. When that happens and you are questioned about the true state of affairs, tell the truth. You are under no obligation to protect a bad boss. You harm the organization you care about if you do. Truly bad bosses do not belong in law enforcement. They are too costly for everyone.

Many more bosses are not easily categorized. They are a little bit of one kind or another in combination. There are always exceptions to the rule, too. A veteran boss may be an incorrigible worrier; a new boss may be comfortably self-confident and a terrific work partner for you. Never forget that there are plenty of really great bosses out there. Like you, every boss has a unique personality. Almost all have at least some positive traits. You can learn from virtually all of them, even if it is something you promise yourself never to do. Indeed, there are all kinds of bosses.

WORKING FOR A DIFFICULT BOSS

Unusual is the individual who honestly can state that he or she has never worked for a difficult boss. Unfortunately, there are more than a few of them out there. Their "difficulties" run the scale, ranging from the simply irritating to the truly vile. And, as already noted, most are not difficult *all* of the time. Your challenge is to work with all of them acceptably and productively well without diluting your effectiveness and your ethics as a leader.

All the same, it is important to remember that the vast majority of leaders you will encounter in policing are not greatly unlike you. They are trying to do a difficult job to the best of their ability. Like you, they have worries, fears, egos, and internal conflicts. But they are laboring, like you, to be good leaders in an important, people-helping cause. Most of them are good people.

You may be fortunate enough never to encounter a really difficult supervisor throughout your career. In today's profession called law enforcement that possibility gets higher all the time. But what if you *do* run across one of these difficult characters? What then? What are the symptoms of a difficult boss? What do they do to make your job and life harder? Why are they difficult bosses?

Bad boss behavior can show up in almost endless varieties. It may be seen in a grump who yells at his subordinates and disrespects employees. Another bad boss may play favorites with employees, elevating a pal to near-saintly status while treating a disliked individual as the department goat. Another bad boss may engage in unethical, immoral, or even unlawful behavior, while yet another may practice sexual harassment or racial bias (which is also unlawful.) The bad boss may be a liar or he may take credit that rightfully belongs to someone else. A bad boss may be an actual, scheming tyrant or simply someone who is disconnected and disinterested in what his subordinates are doing. A bad boss may be just rude or outright venomous.

A bad boss can be one of the above or a combination of several of them. A truly difficult boss is one you do not want to work for. But reality says that one day you may have to, like it or not. If that is your lot, and it well may be, there are some things you can do to at least mitigate the discomfort while you still get your job done competently. These responses have worked for others. None of them comes with a guarantee of radically changing difficult boss behavior but they *can* make your boss relationship better. These difficult boss antidotes include:

- Minimize contact. It does not solve the problem long-term, but it does reduce the aggravation. The key is doing it without looking like you're doing it so that the avoidance is not apparent to your boss. You must be careful not to extend this tactic to the point that it diminishes your effectiveness as a supervisor. The tactic also should be considered a temporary, first aid approach until a more long-lasting fix can come about.
- Seek the advice of your peers. Some of your colleagues may have been dealing with the problem boss a lot longer than you have. They may be able to share with you how they have dealt with the problem, successfully or otherwise, even if it is only to discover the boss's hot buttons and avoid them whenever possible. Reach out quietly. Some discreet conversations with your peers may prove helpful.
- Talk it out. Believe it or not, some bad bosses don't realize that they are bad bosses. They actually do not catch onto the fact that their behavior hurts others. As noted previously, keep your emotions in check and choose a time to meet privately with your boss in a quiet moment when he or she is not unusually stressed or pressured for time. The conversation might begin with you letting your supervisor know what is troubling you. It might go like this: "Boss, I know you would never intentionally

hurt me but I feel really put down when you _____." (Fill in the blank with whatever is making you crazy.) You have thereby given the boss a face-saving way out. He didn't *realize* what he was doing. It's not really his fault, after all. It was up to you to have said something earlier. It is at least partially *your* fault. Or something like that. Naturally, this approach won't work every time with every difficult boss. But it is worth a try. Even if he denies all blame and gets mad, even if he denies any knowledge of what you are talking about, you may have succeeded in changing his behavior for the better. Time will tell. The tactic has worked before to mitigate bad boss behavior. It just might work for you. If the boss repeats his bad behavior in the future, seek him out and quietly and politely bring it to his attention again. Your cumulative action may have more impact on future boss behavior than either of you realize at the moment. There is some discomfort and risk in taking such a direct approach. But you won't be proud of yourself if you do not do *something*. You have to be the ultimate judge of your situation and what to do about it, but the sad fact is that bad behavior that is not confronted is unlikely to change.

- Offer to help. If it is evident to you that certain tasks are especially challenging and upsetting your boss, consider offering to take the task on for him. You might just earn some gratitude and better boss behavior because of your generosity. It is worth a try.
- Don't allow your supervisor's bad behavior to affect your own boss behavior. Oftentimes subordinates mimic their leader's behavior without even realizing they are doing it. Don't let it happen to you if your boss is treating you badly. Your team members do not deserve to be treated in the way your boss may be treating you. Monitor your own behavior and temperament. Never emulate the bad behavior that you receive from a leader. You are better than that.
- Ask for a change. Asking for a reassignment to move away from a bad boss is nearing the nuclear option, the last resort. It should be tried only when you absolutely cannot tolerate the boss behavior any longer. It will, of course, arouse the curiosity of your boss and, likely, that of his boss, as well. Almost certainly you will be asked why you are requesting the change. Realize that some uncomfortable moments may follow your request. True,

that should not happen. After all, you have done nothing wrong. But those moments are likely to come anyway. All the same, life is too short to be miserable all the time, if that is indeed your case. Think it through in an unemotional moment before you make the decision to request the change. Listen to what your good common sense and your feel for organizational survival are telling you. Then, make your decision and go with it.

The reality that your boss (like you) is not without flaw does not mean that the two of you cannot work together. Far from it. Most likely you will have to unless you want to take some drastic measures. (Homicide is not among them.) If you go to work someplace else, there is no guarantee that you won't run into another difficult supervisor. By learning more about your boss, his strengths as well as shortcomings, and what you can do to work around his less-desirable characteristics you may be able to improve your current situation to the point of making it acceptable. You may be able to improve things to the extent that you can accomplish your mission as an effective leader. It is one more example of your talent for problem-solving.

THE RELATIONSHIP YOU BOTH WANT AND NEED

Both you and your boss need to carry out your duties and support the department's mission. You want to do it as effectively and painlessly as possible. Both of you want to look good while doing it. There's no shame in that—looking competent helps you advance your career. You can do good even as you help your team, yourself, and your profession. You and your boss require a good working relationship to aid you in accomplishing all of those things.

As you have already heard repeatedly, mutual trust between the two of you is vital to the working relationship. Trust is gained and built through frequent exposure to the other person, and thereby to his beliefs, character, and personality. Familiarity doesn't breed contempt. It can build trust. Assuming for the moment that your boss is neither a terrorist or a tyrant, spending time with him or her when you can will aid each of you in getting to know (and trust) the other. Certainly, the two of you have plenty of other things to do and you don't have to see each other every day, but spending some time just conversing when there is not a major issue at hand can greatly strengthen the relationship.

Each of you should have the other's back. That begins with the sharing of information on happenings in the somewhat different worlds that you each inhabit. You probably can let him in on the operational side of things. He should be able to enlighten you about what higher leadership is thinking and planning. Each of you will be better equipped to lead with the additional knowledge. Sharing also requires that you both exchange your information completely openly without shading the truth.

Granted, you really cannot control what your boss does or does not do to further the relationship. But there are plenty of things that you do have control over and can make happen. It is up to your boss to reciprocate. You can do things like:

- Volunteer to assume certain of his tasks for him. He likely will appreciate the help and it will give you the opportunity to exhibit your good work. In the process you will be learning your boss's job.
- Prove your credibility and reliability time and again by what you tell your supervisor as well as by your dependability in getting your assignments done correctly and on time. That will result in credit to your account in the boss's bank.
- Don't surprise or embarrass your boss. It is important enough to state again. Keep him in the know about problems or situations that may come to his attention through other channels if you do not inform him first. Assure that your personal actions never result in your boss having to apologize for you. That could mean death to a superior-subordinate relationship. If something bad happens anyway, be sure you are quick with an honest explanation and an apology.
- Always give your best. Never do an assignment for your boss halfway. Your goal should be that your supervisor does not have to return your work product for cleanup or additional work. Like you, your boss has other things to do and is unlikely to appreciate the added delay. But realize also that you cannot read your boss's mind and sometimes he will want you to revise something to suit his particular likes and dislikes. (These you will learn over time if you are observant.)

- Never show fear or self-doubt. Your boss, like your troops, needs to view you as a strong, self-confident leader. You must be careful not to allow self-assurance to stray into perceived arrogance, but you should ensure that your supervisor develops absolute confidence in your demonstrated decision-making and leadership abilities. Fear is catching, but so is demonstrated personal courage. Your boss can gain strength from watching you in action. That is a good thing for the both of you.
- Figure out what your boss needs. Like you, your boss may not always let on when he or she needs assistance. By watching him or her in action you may get some ideas about what you can do to help. Then, ask if you can assist with a particular duty or assignment. The boss is likely to be favorably impressed even if he does not immediately accept help. The added benefit for you once again is that you are learning a piece of your boss's job that may prove helpful to your own career. Everybody wins.
- Defend him, when necessary. Sometimes you are unfairly attacked, as often as not through the spread of inaccurate or biased information. It can happen to your boss, too. Nothing says you should come to his defense when he clearly has done wrong. Your ethics do not permit that. But you don't want to participate in the hanging ahead of the trial. Absent confirmation of your boss's "guilt," speak up and defend your supervisor. You must do that for him if you expect him to do the same for you. It is the right and just thing to do. When your boss finds out you have done it (he'll likely find out if you joined in with the critics, too) you will have bolstered your supervisor's trust in you.

SUMMARY

The relationship you nurture with your boss will have a lot to do with your success (or lack of same) as a leader. Ideally there will exist an atmosphere of trust and actual camaraderie between the two of you. That state of affairs will make your own job easier. But you can be a highly effective leader even under the supervision of a boss who has more than his or her share of faults. You accomplish that by remaining respectful, loyal, and focused on the job at hand. You get your work done well with or without your boss's help. But with some additional effort on your part you increase the chances that you will have that help.

You probably did not get to choose your boss. As a consequence, you will need to learn as much as you can about him in order to be aware of his strengths, weaknesses, interests, eccentricities, and hot buttons. That knowledge should help you boost your own effectiveness by aiding you in avoiding some conflicts with your supervisor. Nevertheless, you always honestly will tell your boss what he needs to know even if you are aware that his hearing it will result in pyrotechnics. It remains your job to look out for your boss's welfare as well as that of the organization as a whole and the community beyond it. That is what a loyal subordinate—and an effective leader—does.

Most law enforcement bosses are ethical, reasonable people. Yours probably does not expect more from you than you do from your own subordinates. Give him or her your best work at all times. Do not try to undermine what he is attempting to accomplish. Trust him unless he proves you can't. Do not speak ill of him in front of others. Remain loyal in the face of adversity. Do your part to make the relationship work well for the both of you. You will be a more effective leader for your efforts—so will your boss.

Chapter 4

MAKING THE TOUGH CALLS

Every conscious human being makes decisions countless times every day. You do, too. Do you want fries with that? Do I have time to get through that yellow light? Is it time for bed? As a law enforcement officer, you make decisions that oftentimes have considerably more gravity. Do I have probable cause for arrest? Do I have enough assistance on-scene? What do I do if this guy runs from me? As someone appointed by your employer to lead others, you have even more critical decisions to make. Do we force entry or wait? Is it time to halt the vehicle pursuit? Is lethal force appropriate in this situation?

Your agency relies on you to make consistently sound decisions. Your perceived ability to do that is likely the primary reason you were promoted to leadership rank. Your team members expect the same. So, how do you do it? How do you make the really tough calls?

There are a number of tactics and techniques you can apply in your quest to arrive at a timely, effective decision in your role as a law enforcement leader. There are some time-proven things you can do, even when you don't know what to do. First it may prove helpful to take a look at some common obstacles to good decision-making.

THE ENEMIES OF SOUND DECISION-MAKING

There is no doubt that as a law enforcement leader you are tasked with making critical, sometimes life-changing decisions to go along with the many more "routine" ones you make every day. In your chosen profession the consequences of a bad or delayed decision can have much graver consequences than in most other lines of work. Oftentimes when decisions go wrong the error can be traced back to one or more contributing, causative factors. Factors such as:

- NOISE. This one also could be referred to as distractions from the decision-making process. It can mean the commotion at the scene of a critical incident or the emotional and mental distractions that may be interfering with your decision-making concentration. Whichever is the case, if feasible you need to get away from the noise to the extent possible in order to make a good decision.
- RUSHING. Yes, emergency situations may require an immediate decision from you so that disaster can be averted. But more often you will have at least *some* time to take a few deep breaths, gather information, and *think* before you act. Rushing when the situation does not justify great speed can detract from the quality of your decision-making. Do your best to avoid unnecessary speed.
- PROCRASTINATION. It could be considered the polar opposite of rushing unnecessarily. Waiting too long, putting off a decision for more and more information and consideration also can be highly damaging to effective decision-making. Sometimes a decision delayed without good cause can cause a lot of harm. Putting it off because it is uncomfortable is unlikely to make it easier. The imperfect decision is almost always better that none at all. Go ahead and make it when it is your responsibility to do so.
- PERSONAL BIAS OR PREJUDICE. If you already have shaded your view of the situation requiring decision-making through your own likes and dislikes your decision may not be as reliable as one you make with an open mind. For example, if you have already decided that probable cause exists for an arrest based upon the skin color of the suspect, you are headed for trouble. Everyone harbors personal biases, to one degree or another. Be conscious of yours and try to keep them out of your decision-making.
- PERSONAL EMOTIONAL INVOLVEMENT. This one may be closely related to the display of personal emotions and biases. In law enforcement you are constantly required to keep your emotions in check, as hard as that may be at times. Do an emotional self-inventory before you make a tough call. Be certain

that your personal feelings are not influencing your decision-making.

- TRYING TOO HARD TO PLEASE EVERYONE. It is probably not possible, anyhow. As you know, the world (and your own organization) contains critics and self-appointed experts who are going to second-guess your decisions no matter what call you make. You cannot be paralyzed into failing to make a decision because of that reality. Give it your best shot and try to let go. Chances are you did just fine.
- GOING IT ALONE. Some decision-making will happen so quickly that you will have to handle it all by yourself. You are clearly capable of doing that. But that will not always be the case. Other times there will be nothing wrong with running your planned decision by a colleague, or several of them. A peer may detect something you missed. He may have faced a similar decision in the past. When it is practical, there can be great strength in collective decision-making.
- HESITANCY TO ALTER THE STATUS QUO. Doing something other than what has been done before can require courage. You have plenty of that commodity. Don't be afraid to try something new. Sometimes innovation is the right answer. Do not hesitate to give it a try. Your courage is showing, you know.
- DON'T IGNORE HISTORY. Has a similar situation requiring decision-making arisen before? What was done at that time? How well did it work? Knowing something about what has gone before may help you make a tough call today. If there is time, tap your peers' memories as well as your own. Recalling history also may tell you of what not to try. The world is changing and sometimes the right answers change along with it.
- FAILING TO CONSIDER ALL THE EVIDENCE. If you only take into account the information that supports your favored decision you may miss some important points and end up with something short of a sound, evidence-based decision. Slow down just a little and examine all the known facts and circumstances. Do it minus a preconceived notion of what the decision-making outcome should be. You are almost certain to make a better call.
- FAILING TO BENEFIT FROM EXPERIENCE. You get better at making decisions by making decisions. You have heard that

before and it is true. Learning from what has happened in the past will help you better handle what happens in the future. That includes making the really tough calls. You learn from the losses at least as much as you do from the wins. Keep mental note of your past decisions and their repercussions. You will do even better in the future.

The enemies to sound decision-making can have value. They can teach you a lot. Make full use of them in making the tough calls that will come tomorrow and the day after that. Avoid them like you would the mystery meat at the all-night greasy spoon.

THE ELEMENTS OF A GOOD DECISION

As a leader you are expected to make good decisions. That is a given. You also must avoid the roadblocks to sound decision-making that you just read about. But just what is involved in making all of those good decisions that you are expected to make? A number of key elements are called for and they include the following:

KNOWLEDGE AND INFORMATION. To make a sound decision you first need to have as much solid information as possible on the situation you are addressing. That likely involves researching the circumstances in depth in the time that you have available before you must reach a decision. You would like to know such things as:

- What are the known, confirmed facts of the situation or incident?
- Who are the players?
- Are there time constraints on your decision-making? If so, what are they?
- What limits or parameters must you work within while reaching a decision and acting on it? Policies, laws, and your boss's directions may be examples of common constraints.
- Is history helpful? What has happened previously that may impact what you can do now?
- Where can you get help, assuming there is time for that? Is there human (fellow supervisors) or documentary (policies and procedures) assistance that might help you? It is likely that others have faced an identical or similar situation before. Try to find out what they did and how well it worked.

YOUR INTELLIGENCE AND TRAINING. In order to make a good decision you need to know your business inside and out. Yours is law enforcement leadership. That solid base of knowledge and training will help you "stay on the rails" as you travel towards a sound decision. That's one more reason why you must never cease expanding your education and training data base.

COMMON SENSE. There it is again. Your street smarts and life experience will help you stay on track if you use them wisely. If your common sense is telling you that something is a bad idea, try something else instead. Believe that little voice inside your head. It is likely speaking from experience.

GOOD JUDGMENT. Likely it is heavily influenced by decisions, good and bad, that you have made previously. Judgment is built through courage married to common sense. Good judgment calls for self-confidence and decisiveness, allied elements required for solid decision-making. Your observed good judgment was another of the reasons your employer selected you for promotion from the ranks. Don't hesitate to rely on it.

PERSONAL COURAGE. Sometimes your reaching a decision will anger or disappoint someone, or a number of them. Unfortunately, that is among the consequences of decision-making. You will need to have and exercise the backbone required to make the tough calls, even when it means someone will not be happy with your call. That doesn't mean that you should take pleasure in making others unhappy. It just means you will need the courage to go ahead and make the call even when you know in advance that others will disagree and be disappointed.

EMPATHY FOR THOSE AFFECTED. A great leader has an appreciation for the feelings of others, most especially when it comes to how they are impacted by that leader's decisions. Empathy is a commodity that every exceptional leader has in good supply. You will need to apply yours to those affected by your decisions. Yes, you have the courage required to make unpopular decisions. But you also have sincere empathy for those affected by those decisions. You are a human being with a human's emotions. That's how it should be with an exceptional leader.

WILLINGNESS TO LISTEN TO OTHERS. You are smart enough to know that you are not the only one capable of having good ideas. Someone else may have a solution to a problem you are facing, or may at least have information that will help you solve it. You won't know that, however, unless you are willing to keep an open ear and a ready mind attuned to the thoughts and ideas of others. A good leader spends at least as much time listening as he does in talking. You can learn a lot that way. You *may* even learn exactly what you need to make a tough call.

TIMELINESS. Seldom will you have all of the time you would like to have to reach a decision regarding a tough call. On occasion you may have only seconds. Whatever the case, you must master the art of thinking on your feet with the goal of consistently making the right call in the limited time you have available. More often than not the first solution you arrive at will be a good one. Putting a whole lot more time into pondering it probably will not guarantee a much more satisfactory resolution. Understand what time constraints you are working under. Then, do your best to work within them on your way to making that tough call.

GRASP OF CONSEQUENCES. Try to thoroughly evaluate before you make the call what the results of your decision will be. What will be the impact on the various people affected by the call? Attempt to minimize the "unanticipated consequences" of your decision-making. By thoroughly thinking through in the time you have available your decision and its consequences for other people you may be able to mitigate or even eliminate the unexpected results. At the same time, be ready to alter your decision if unanticipated consequences say that you should. A good leader is nothing if not flexible. Revisions to your initial decision are acceptable and sometimes absolutely required.

CLEAR COMMUNICATION. Anyone and everyone who might be even remotely interested in or affected by your decision needs to know what you, the leader, has decided. Oftentimes that calls for repetition of your message. The message (decision) itself may need put into both written and oral formats, but it absolutely must be made clear to everyone whose well-being, effectiveness, and efficiency depends on it. Do not keep your decision a secret from those who need to know it.

Sound decisions don't just happen. They are carefully crafted by exceptional leaders after considerable mental effort. Exceptional leaders like you.

WHEN YOU DON'T KNOW WHAT TO DO

No matter how smart you are, no matter how extensive your training and depth of experience, you are going to confront a situation on the job that you have not been formally prepared to handle. You are going to be required to make decisions, perhaps quick ones, about things you have not encountered previously. On occasion you, like Kirk and Spock, are going to be going where no one has gone before. Or at least that is the way it may seem to you, the man or woman expected to make sense of it all and arrive at a sound decision. The good news is that you as a highly-competent leader can do it, and do it well.

There are some helpful guidelines you should be aware of when you don't know what to do next. Guidelines like:

- There are few absolutes. You probably learned in the academy that there are things that you must *always* do and things that you must *never* do. These were absolutes. That is true, to a point. For example, you never want to fail to search someone you have taken into lawful custody. But experience has taught you that there are far fewer absolutes than you once may have been led to believe. If it works and it is lawful and ethical and safe it's hard to say that it was the wrong thing to do. Keep that in mind when you are faced with a decision that reveals no one, proven, established route to solution. Something that someone has never tried before just might be the right route to take. After all, it worked for Captain Kirk!
- There are even fewer flawless decisions. Few things in the world are absolutely without imperfections. Decisions are found among those things. If the decision you make when faced with a situation for which no "traditional" response worked, so be it. A perfect decision was not mandated. A fair, ethical, legal one that worked was. Be content with that fact and consider it a tough call well made.
- When possible, slow down a bit. Again: you may not be able to do that in the maw of a major, life-threatening crisis. But if you can, even a little slowing can help you arrive at the best call. Give your thought processes time to take hold and your creative juices to flow. You are apt to arrive at a better decision for a never-before-encountered dilemma.

- Deep breaths can help. As you slow down, remind yourself to take several slow, deep breaths. Doing that is likely to help calm you. The added oxygen will benefit your body and feed your brain. In the process you just might come up with a fresh solution to a novel set of circumstances.
- Step back and away. It is possible to be so close to and intimately involved with a challenge that you can fail to see the bigger picture and along with it some possible responses. That can happen in decision-making, too. Putting just a little distance between yourself and a tough, novel problem may help you seize upon a solution. That calls for thinking about something else, at least for a time. Doing that may help you see the proverbial forest that's beyond the single, fat tree that is obstructing your vision. Whenever there is time try it and see if you think and decide better after a short timeout.
- Call once more on your common sense and life experience. What feels like a good answer to the question you are facing? What does your common sense, that little inner voice, tell you to do? You may have had the right answer all along without realizing it. A decision may be there, just beyond your immediate reach in the back of your mind. Be courageous enough to reach back there for it.
- Keep things in perspective. You may be facing a life or death matter, or something close to it. But many of the decisions you will be called upon to make, even those for which you initially have no answer, are probably not vital to the survival of the planet. Realize that the world probably isn't going to end if you don't get it just right. More than a few things that felt like a pending disaster on Monday morning are forgotten by Friday afternoon.
- Don't wait too long to get help. Your ego may tell you that you need to make this novel decision all by yourself. That desire may cause you to wait too long to seek the assistance that you truly need. There is no shame in asking for help when you need it. You would expect your subordinates to call for help when needed. In fact, you probably feel a little bit honored that they asked. Your peers probably look at it the same way. Ask for help when you are stumped by a really tough call. You may find that your "helpers" seek your advice, in turn.

- Be willing to revise your approach. You have floated your trial balloon. You have sent your decision up the flagpole and nobody has saluted it. In other words, your first try at solving the problem you are facing does not seem to be working, or at least not working as well as you want. From what you have seen or experienced so far, is it possible that a modification to your original decision might be helpful? Don't be afraid to give it a try if a change in your initial decision may have a chance of working better. It does not show weakness or indecisiveness to alter a decision that looks like could be improved. It *would* show foolishness not to learn from what is happening and be ready to tweak your first decision.
- Do it and go on. It is possible but unwise to agonize endlessly over a tough call you had to make, especially if the results did not approach perfection. It is human to do so but it is not helpful, nonetheless. When you don't know what to do, just do your best with what you have been given to work with. Adjust and improve your call if that is indicated and possible. Then, move on with life—and decision-making. There is almost certainly another decision in your future that will not be accompanied by a set of instructions on how to make it. Look forward and not back. Learn as you go and get ready for the next one.

LEARNING BY EXPERIENCE

Experience. It is probably the most reliable means for learning that exists. You get better for the future by recalling what happened in the past. That principle applies to making the tough calls, the really hard decisions. You get better by remembering and then doing. Oftentimes it works. Other times it doesn't. You learn from those less-than-ideal decisions, too.

It is a good idea to ask trusted others to critique your decision-making. Do that in addition to the self-critique that you conduct. How is your tough decision working out? Are there negative or unintended consequences, good or bad? Can making an adjustment to the initial decision make it better? For example, your decision to alter the shift hours for the overnight Patrol watch looked great before it was implemented. Now, with your decision in place, your troops are reporting problems with what they see as an overly-complex and hard to understand work schedule. A couple of officers have even made suggestions for changes that may allow for it to work better. You must be smart as well as humble enough to analyze their input and, if indicated, implement their suggested revisions.

Good ideas don't come only from supervisors. As you may have been quick to tell others back when you were a frontline officer, oftentimes the best ideas come from those who are closest to the work. It is true. Your subordinates' opinions on your decisions should be considered, too. What they have to say based upon their real-world observations may help you make your decision an even better one.

It also may prove useful to examine your decision over a longer time period, whether that means hours or months of careful observation. It might take a while for those pesky unintended consequences to come to light. For instance, the new, longer shifts are showing a number of benefits, including better coverage on the street and a boost in officer morale due to the longer time off. But over time the use of sick leave and on-the-job accidents have both climbed steadily. Is there a correlation? Further examination is indicated. A revision to the decision may be in order. Do not let your pride or fear of criticism keep you from altering a decision that the evidence plainly shows needs revised. Your ample courage needs to be applied here, too. Always be open to changing your mind and your decision when the facts say you should. It is what mature, self-confident leaders do.

Just as you get better at making traffic stops by making traffic stops, you should continue to get better at decision-making as you make decisions throughout your leadership career. It is important that you review each tough call in a quiet moment and examine what went well and what can be improved upon. What did the experience teach? How can the lesson be applied to the next time the opportunity to make a hard decision presents itself? You safely can wager that the next opportunity isn't too far distant.

SUMMARY

You get better at just about anything by doing it—a lot. It just follows that the more tough calls you make, the more competent and comfortable you will become in making them. Building experience in tough decision-making leads to making better tough decisions. You are aware of the components of good decision-making. Included are the required elements of good common sense, empathy, integrity, courage, sound judgment, open-mindedness, and the willingness to accept input from others who might assist you.

You are equally aware of the decision-making enemies that can dilute the effectiveness of your timely decision-making. You know by now that these bugaboos include procrastination, unnecessary rushing, personal bias, and an aversion to trying anything new. All of these decision detractors you can overcome through the application of your courage, solid common sense, and sound judgment.

You also have learned by experience that there are sources of help you can reach out to when you are uncertain about what to do in a given situation. Your experience additionally has taught you that if it works, it works. It is hard to argue with success. Experience likewise has taught you that every decision you make does not have to be perfect. If you solved the problem by making the tough call, you have done your job well. That holds true even if someone else would have done it differently. Remember that when an armchair quarterback spouts off about "what I would have done."

Your employer counts on you to make the tough calls. It is one of your most important responsibilities as a leader. Sometimes you have to make those calls under extremely adverse conditions within severe time constraints. But you make them all the same. That's what great leaders do.

Chapter 5

TACTICAL DECISION-MAKING

Every day in these United States law enforcement leaders make thousands of decisions concerning tactical situations. Those tactical problems can range from a building search for an armed bad guy to a mass shooting incident to a terrorist attack. Almost all of these decisions are good ones, which provides solid evidence of the professional competence of you and your peers. On the rare occasions where they do not go well you can be assured of widespread criticism by the media and the rest of the self-appointed "experts." Such is the life of a law enforcement leader.

The truth is that you do it right most of the time. Not infrequently that is because of the tactical know-how and common sense you apply to a field problem when there isn't a carefully-outlined "book answer" to be had. Like the first-line leaders and grunts who saved the D-Day landings in Normandy after the carefully-laid plans began to fall apart, that's when you are at your courageous best. That's when you truly shine at decision-making under fire, perhaps in the literal sense.

But, being you, you always want to get better. That's good. That makes law enforcement better. That saves lives. There are some very basic steps you can take to resolve successfully any tactical challenge you are facing. They can help you get even better. It all starts with careful analysis of the tactical challenge blocking your path.

ANALYZING THE PROBLEM

There are a lot of things you will need to learn about the tactical problem you are facing in the time you have available to learn them.

Securing the answers to as many of the questions as possible will aid you in arriving at a safe and sound solution. You will want answers to such questions as:

- What has happened so far?
- Who are the actors?
- What are the *known* threats?
- Are there time constraints? What are they?
- What are your resources?
- What aid do you need, including specialized personnel and equipment?
- What is the outcome you are seeking? (It is not necessarily evident.)
- What laws, policies, and procedures apply to this situation?
- Are there complications that will make reaching a satisfactory resolution more difficult?
- What *don't* you know about the situation that could prove hazardous?

Every incident will, of course, be unique in the challenges it poses even if it is similar to something you have faced before. Nevertheless, your previous experience likely will prove very helpful in finding a solution to the present problem. Mine your memory for what it can tell you.

Naturally, the preparations and decisions you will make to resolve a barricaded gunman incident will not be identical to the ones you will employ at the scene of a major transportation disaster. But there are basic actions you can take that will apply to one extent or another to virtually any tactical problem. They include the following:

Assess the situation. Do a quick size-up of what you are confronting. Reach out to those already on-scene for what they may be able to tell you. Rely on your own senses and observations, too. Beware of rumors and unconfirmed reports. Act on facts. Try to determine what may happen next. Keep track of the important questions that you have been unable to answer, such as whether or not a barricaded suspect has someone inside with him. You may be able to answer them over time.

Take command. Especially early on in a tactical incident law enforcement personnel may be unsure of who is in charge. There may be several well-intentioned people giving perhaps conflicting orders. Worse, no one may have assumed command. If someone else is clearly and competently in charge, let them know you are there to help in a subordinate role. Ask for your assignment. Otherwise, take charge and assure that everyone who needs to know is aware of it. Establish a command post or center and be sure everyone knows where it is, even if it is only the interior of a police vehicle. You will want representatives of all assisting entities present at the post.

Develop an initial action plan. You will prioritize the problems you are aware of and address the most critical—the most life-threatening—first. Be prepared to alter your plans quickly should the situation change or as you learn additional information. Flexibility should be your watchword as you plan, make decisions, and execute a response.

Issue clear directions. You must voice clear, concise, and direct orders to those who are assisting you in handling a critical incident. Encourage clarifying questions to be sure everyone knows what is expected of him or her. You should ask questions of your people to be certain that they understand what they are supposed to be doing.

Get all required assistance. Your initial and ongoing assessments should help you determine what additional help you will require to safely handle any and all threats. Get it on the way now. Realize that your requirements may change as the situation changes and you make additional decisions. Also realize that it is always preferable to request extra help as opposed to too little. You always can send away surplus aid if it turns out to be unneeded. Once more, flexibility is the key. Continue to re-assess and revise as necessary.

Share what you know. Information sharing is vital. Be certain that you keep everyone involved briefed as to the current situation and what is expected to happen next. Expect the other players to keep you, the coach, advised of relevant information they become aware of. This is not a time to keep secrets.

Be prepared to relinquish control. A long-running tactical incident may require you to pass command to your relief, or to the commander of a specialized unit. You must not attempt to stay in control past the point that fatigue sets in. That's when less-than-ideal decisions get made. Stay fresh and sharp for the next decision point. When an exchange of command takes place assure that you pass along via a detailed briefing everything that you know about what has transpired so far. Encourage and respond to questions. Realize, too, that you will have to arrange for the relief of your personnel before fatigue begins to sap their effectiveness. Always keep the human factor in mind as you make your tactical decisions.

Don't overlook the people. A major tactical situation or critical incident can have a huge mental and emotional impact on all of those involved. Post Traumatic Stress Disorder is very real. Particularly when a tactical situation involves serious injury or death, you and your people could later develop symptoms that indicate the incident may have a more lasting impact than initially realized. Keep an eye on yourself and others for persistent changes in on- or off-duty behavior and demeanor. Signs that something isn't quite right could range from nightmares, inability to sleep, depression, sexual dysfunctions, physical illnesses, and more. Skilled, professional intervention is indicated if those symptoms continue. Emotional injuries can be every bit as serious as physical ones. Do not neglect your own emotional or mental welfare or that of your troops.

Witnesses and victims may require the assistance of professional trauma and grief counselors. Law enforcement officers may need the assistance of a police psychologist or peer support group. As a decision-maker you should offer services to all who may require it. No stigma should be attached to the need for special assistance. Never overlook the reality that you—the decision-maker—may need professional help, too. Do not hesitate to get the help you need. You owe it to yourself as well as those you lead and those at home who care about you.

Plan for demobilization. Even before the tactical situation is finally resolved you should be making plans to release no longer needed resources to be returned to other duties. That might include personnel and equipment brought in from other agencies. It additionally may be necessary to get evacuees back home. Those affected should be advised of the resolution of the tactical situation as soon as possible. They will be highly anxious to return to their interrupted lives. Demobilization also should include plans for a debriefing session for the personnel involved. It may need to be delayed until those involved have rested up, but take place it must so that learning can occur. The format for this session could be an informal chat over coffee for a handful of people to a full-scale meeting held in a classroom with audiovisual support.

BASIC PRINCIPLES OF PROBLEM-SOLVING

There are specific tactical responses for specific tactical situations. There are also specific steps you can take when meeting any tactical challenge. These basic principles of tactical problem-solving include the following:

LEARN AS MUCH AS YOU CAN ABOUT WHAT YOU ARE FACING. You cannot solve the problem, tactical or otherwise, until you identify it along with all its component parts. Gather all of the reliable information that you have time to collect before you make your informed decision.

APPLY ALL OF YOUR JOB KNOWLEDGE AND EXPERIENCE. Everything you know about your profession and all your past experiences have helped prepare you to make this tactical call. Review what you know and make the decision.

GET HELP IF THERE'S TIME. You may not have to go it alone. Someone else—a peer, subordinate, or superior—may have sound advice that will aid you in your tactical decision-making. You won't know if you don't ask for assistance. Do not let your ego get in the way of devising a good solution to a tactical challenge.

EXERCISE YOUR PERSONAL COURAGE. It takes courage to take a risk and apply a decision that may or may not work. Tactical decision-making sometimes requires going out on a limb and trying a novel approach to a situation. You have that kind of courage.

ACCEPT OWNERSHIP OF THE DECISION. Whether it is a crazed shooter in a shopping mall or an angry grandma with a big knife, a dangerous scenario has been placed in your lap for a safe resolution. Make your best call. Do not attempt to lay it off on someone else. Accept it as your own. That is displaying both responsibility and personal courage, both of which you have in good supply.

BE WILLING TO TAKE ACCEPTABLE RISKS. It goes along with personal courage and owning your decisions. The key word is *acceptable*. Unnecessary and reckless risks to innocent others should never be a part of your tactical decision-making. Make a carefully-measured decision. Assess the actual risk level before you act. Realize that in your business very few things can be made totally risk-free.

EXERCISE PATIENCE. Your solution to a tactical problem may not be immediately apparent. Or it may not work on the first try. You may need a lot of patience to get it done right. Don't give up. Take some deep breaths, back up, and try again.

SHOW COMPASSION AND EMPATHY. Your decision-making almost certainly will affect others, perhaps in a life-changing way. Do what the facts indicate that you should do. But never overlook the feelings and concerns of those your decision will affect. Provide emotional support where you can.

DEMONSTRATE THE ABILITY TO PRIORITIZE AND TRIAGE WISELY. Your tactical situation may present you with several threats and multiple problems, all at the same time. You will need the ability to place these issues in the appropriate order for decisions and solutions. They are unlikely to all be of the same level of criticality. Deal with the most important and the most dangerous first.

BE FLEXIBLE. Sometimes you will need to depend upon your ability and willingness to backtrack and try something else if your first solution falls short. You likewise will have to be willing to improvise on the fly when unanticipated complications arise. Try not to get mentally locked into a single solution. There may be other avenues to try.

BE OPEN TO LEARNING. You can learn from your failures as well as your successes. Mistakes perhaps more than victories can have powerful teaching abilities. Take each experience in and lodge it in your personal memory bank for the next time you encounter something similar.

DISPLAY SINCERE MODESTY. Yes, modesty. It's great that you solved your tactical crisis, but it is unlikely that you accomplished the feat all by yourself. Be certain that you award credit where credit is due. Modesty is becoming in a great leader.

All of the preceding are principles that you can apply to virtually any decision-making exercise. But when the crisis you are facing is a tactical one there are yet other considerations to keep in mind on the way to an "everyone goes home" solution. Consider these guidelines for effective (and safe) tactical decision-making whenever suspects are part of the scenario:

- Begin gathering information well before you arrive on-scene. Learn everything you can from your dispatcher and anyone else who may have relevant information. That information could include such data as:
  Number and description of suspects/victims/witnesses?

Is their identity known?
Weapons involved? What kind?
Last known location of suspects?
Are there injuries? How serious?
Offenses believed involved?
Description and layout of the location involved?
Any other known threats?

And, of course, there is the biggest question of all: What *don't* I know about this situation that could cause harm to innocent people?

- Plan how you will approach, arrive, and deploy well before you get there. Coordinate your deployment with other responding units. Give clear directions as to where you want your help to go.
- Recall that invisible deployment is the goal in most tactical, crime-in-progress scenarios. You desire to surprise the suspect(s), not have it happen the other way around.
- Constant situational awareness is your ally in safely resolving a tactical problem involving suspects. The greatest threat is the one you did not detect.
- Continue your information gathering. The tactical situation you are handling may be a fluid and constantly changing one. Keep collecting fresh information and be prepared to alter your decisions and responses quickly.
- Establish a command post. You will need a secure, central location where you and your helpers can gather to work on decision-making if the tactical situation is an ongoing one. You do not want to waste precious time chasing down people you need to assist you.
- Take some deep breaths. Seriously. Doing that will help to calm you even as it grants you some time to think, plan, and decide. The slight delay will help your brain gain control over an adrenaline dump. It likely will make the decisions you make and the actions you take better ones.
- Be prepared to act quickly and decisively. It is not often you will have to make a major decision the instant you arrive at a critical incident scene in order to save a life. But it *could* happen any-time. Realize it could happen and be mentally prepared to act

decisively without much time to think. Your quick decision probably will not have to be perfectly flawless. But you nonetheless will have to decide without pause. Be willing and ready to meet the challenge.

- Know that you are likely to face distractions to good decision-making. You well know that most critical incidents are attended by initial pandemonium and confusion. Realize that unwanted help (extra cops, for example), crowds, news media, and other people who want to help or just want to see what's going on quickly will gather, too. Assign one or more of your assistants to corral these folks into a staging area or other spot for press and public. Allowing your workspace to get too crowded will compromise your ability to sort things out and make good decisions. Bringing a reasonable degree of order from disorder is your goal on the way to arriving at a sound decision, or a series of them, in a tactical situation.

You are good at decision-making under pressure. Your skills should not be diminished when the decision to be made is a tactical one. You can do this, and do it well.

WHEN THINGS GO WRONG

Alright. You have made your tactical decision. And it didn't work, or at least it did not as well as you had intended. Now what?

There are few completely perfect decisions or solutions when the problem is a tactical one. There are simply too many intervening factors (including very human ones) for perfection to be guaranteed. If you have at least mitigated the problem or lessened the gravity of the tactical situation you have achieved a degree of success. But, being you, you naturally want to do better than that. That is understandable, too.

You may yet have the opportunity to solve the remaining tactical challenge. Take in what has happened as a result of your initial decision(s). Carefully examine what you know of the results. What can you learn from what you see? Can you alter your approach somewhat and try again? What is the worst that can happen if you changed your first solution and tried again? Unless it appears that your revised response will result in an unacceptable level of risk to innocent others, make the appropriate alterations to your initial decision and response and try again.

Take ownership in your tactical decision-making, imperfect or otherwise. Do not blame others if things did not go exactly as you wanted. If others were, in fact, to blame for the less-than-great outcome, that fact is likely to become evident. You do not need to point it out. Even if the outcome is not perfect, an intelligent boss will credit you for your initiative and willingness to take responsibility.

Speaking of bosses: be sure to keep your chain of command advised of the tactical situation you are handling or have just handled. Your boss, you'll recall, does not like surprises any more than you, particularly if things have not gone according to plan. Do not make your boss reach out to you for a report. You also don't want him or her learning of the results of your decision-making work from someone else. Granted you have a lot more to do than call your supervisor with frequent updates. But keeping the boss in the loop is extremely important. Make time for it.

Yes, things may have gone wrong. Tactical decisions you have made in good faith have not turned out to be flawless ones. But this is not the end of the world. The sun will come up in the morning. There *will* be more tactical decisions to be made tomorrow. Be sure you are mentally ready to do what you do best: lead.

LEARNING FROM OTHERS

You have long known that you can learn a lot about law enforcement by watching and listening to those who have done it longer than you have. You have figured out that you can learn a lot about what not to do by recalling the mistakes made by others. These two principles would appear to be especially applicable to the competent handling of tactical problems.

There is no doubt that you can glean a great deal of knowledge by recalling the experiences of your subordinates, peers, and supervisors. But there are other good sources that should not be overlooked for their educational value. Today more than ever there is a huge volume of information available through law enforcement texts, magazines, journals, and Internet content. The Net has presented a wealth of see-

it-now video that graphically illustrates the results of tactical decisions—both good and bad—made by your law enforcement colleagues
across the nation and the world. Body-worn cameras on cops have
been responsible for much of that real-life drama.

Even staying current with how the news media is portraying law
enforcement officers and their responses to tactical problems can
teach you much. You do not have to like or agree with the narrative
that too often feels anti-cop. You can still learn from much from the
images on your television or computer screen depicting your colleagues doing it right—or wrong. Force yourself, if you must. But do
watch it.

Examining and carefully dissecting tactical decisions that already
have been made can help you prepare for the ones you will have to
make in the future. Do not overlook the learning value to be found in
an after-action critique or debriefing performed following a critical
incident that called for tactical decision-making. The session can be as
formal as one conducted in a meeting room for dozens of people or
as informal as four cops sitting down in an all-night restaurant's corner
booth. The important thing is that the discussion and its opportunity
for learning takes place before time has dimmed the recollections of
the participants.

Such a debriefing should be done in a non-judgmental environment where everyone participating feels free to speak openly and
truthfully. The purpose of the exercise is not to place blame but to
learn how to get better for next time. There is no doubt that the effort
will require courage on you part as a leader, particularly if you are
doubtful or self-conscious about the tactical decisions you made. Take
comfort in the reality that very likely every other debriefing participant is nervous about his or her role in the incident, too. Learning
sometimes brings a little discomfort. You learned that in elementary
school. But the temporary discomfort is almost always worth it for the
knowledge gained. Your ample personal courage should see you
through the session.

In all of this, your goal is never to stop learning. There are things
that others can teach you. Even those not in your profession will on
occasion have valuable input towards the successful resolution of a
police-oriented problem, including a tactical one. It is always worth
hearing what they have to say. You would not turn down an offer from
a citizen to help you control a violent inebriate. The same principle

holds true when the threat arrives in the form of a particularly nasty tactical dilemma.

SUMMARY

There is a very good chance that your recognized ability to make critical decisions in stressful circumstances was one of the main reasons your organization selected you for a leadership role in the first place. If you are like many of your peers, making those decisions in tactical situations, critical incidents, is perhaps the most rewarding part of your job. That's just the kind of leader you are.

Almost certainly you promised yourself earlier in your leadership career that you would never cease in your efforts to get even better at making tactical decisions. That attitude in and of itself will help to make you more competent at tactical decision-making.

But there's more to it, and you have just reviewed some of the basic guidelines involved. Your first step is the careful analysis of the tactical situation you are facing within the time and resource constraints that you are confronting. You next will apply the fundamental principles of problem-solving tailored to meet the special circumstances of law enforcement problems of a tactical nature. You will be prepared to regroup and revise when an initial decision does not result in the desired results. Finally, you will learn from your own experiences and those of others to get ready for the next tactical decision. It is out there waiting to test your decision-making mettle.

In almost everything you do on the job the slogan "everyone goes home" is never out of mind. It governs much of what you do, but never more so than in the face of a tactical situation. When you make a sound tactical decision you help carry out that promise.

To the last minute of your last day on the job you will be a tactical decision-maker. By doing that job well you will protect your people and the citizens you serve. You will be a problem-solver. You will be a leader.

Chapter 6

YOUR RESPONSIBILITIES AS A TRAINER

As a leader yet another of your vital tasks is to help prepare your subordinates for the diverse challenges of what has become a very complex and difficult job: law enforcement. How well you carry out your important assignment will have a major impact on how successful your people are in meeting those challenges in an effective, safe, and compassionate manner.

Today's law enforcer has to be so much more than that. He or she must be a psychological counselor, medic, negotiator, mental health expert, tactical operator, and more. That officer must be expert in technical skills that did not even exist for the law enforcement officers of a generation ago. He must be sensitive to the emotional mood of the country and his own jurisdiction. He must be able to avoid offending the sensibilities of politicians and media types who are quick to find fault with whatever he does, even though doing his difficult job would be far beyond their own abilities. As you well know, it is harder than ever to be a cop in today's world. Anything and everything you can do to ease the burden on your officers will be welcomed by them. You can help accomplish that through relevant, well-presented training.

Some of that education you can handle yourself as a skilled teacher. Identifying exactly what it is that your people need will help you do that. Assembling a helpful lesson plan from which you can conduct your training presentation will contribute greatly to your efforts, as will measuring by testing and observation whether your endeavors were successful.

Doubtlessly your organization relies upon some form of Field Training Officer (FTO) program to help prepare new officers for the difficult job ahead. Other than their first-line supervisors, the FTOs are a rookie officer's most valuable resource for determining what kind of law enforcement practitioner he or she will become. These trainers must be selected carefully for demeanor and loyalty to the organization and profession as well as their technical competency and ability as a teacher. They must be the agency's best. Hopefully you as a leader will have a say in helping choose and prepare them for their vital responsibility as role models. The task is that important to the future of the organization.

As vital as the FTO is, he does not eclipse your importance as the molder of new law enforcement officers. The criticality of your role as trainer and educator cannot be overestimated. Like so many of your other responsibilities, you must do it well. Here's how to go about it.

WHAT SHOULD YOU COVER?

One of your first jobs as a trainer is to determine what it is your people need to better prepare them for their work. You begin with the assumption that all have attended an academy of some kind and received basic law enforcement training. Beyond that their departmental training and experience may vary from the green-as-grass rookie to the saltiest veteran. Their formal education also may range from a high school diploma to post-graduate university work. Their ability and willingness to gain additional knowledge likely will vary, as well. Your team may include the youngster who wants to know *everything* to aid in her upward climb in the department to the older cop nearing retirement who doesn't really want to be bothered with newfangled knowledge. Welcome to the world of the law enforcement trainer!

You can begin your effort to assess your officers' training needs by identifying what is most *relevant* to their assignment. It would make little sense to train a property crimes detective in how to complete a traffic accident investigation, for instance. Beyond that, what do your personal observations tell you? By watching your officers work you may ascertain that certain aspects of their officer safety practices are lacking. You may observe that, say, their efforts at directing traffic are less-than-satisfactory. Do all or most of your people need additional work here, or is it just one or two individuals? Your observations should tell you how best and how widely to address their training needs.

There is another especially valuable means for identifying your peoples' training needs: ask them. Query them individually and as a group. It may take a bit of probing and persistence on your part. Cops are not always the most forthcoming at reporting their lack of anything. Keep at it. You need to know where *they* feel they need work.

What does your state's peace officer licensing authority require periodic updates to cover? What does your agency mandate? See that these needs are covered in any in-service training program you put together. Required training must come first.

If your employer has a risk manager on staff, meet with him or her to get an idea of what he or she sees as a pressing training need for your officers. (Hint: additional defensive driving training may be near the top of the list.) Do the same with your jurisdiction's prosecutors and your employer's civil attorneys. What do they see, based on their experience with your officers, as the greatest need for additional legal training? Then, do your best to enlist all of these experts' assistance in putting on the training your personnel should have. Much if not all of it may have to be conducted in relatively short sessions during roll call briefings. This may make it harder to get busy outside instructors to commit to the time requirement. It is nonetheless worth making the effort to recruit them for the potential benefit for all involved. Realize that you may have to take some of the material and do the training yourself. The good news is that you do not have to do it alone. You should be able to get some of your FTOs, supervisor wannabes, and other outstanding performers on the team or shift to help with the presentations. Some supervisors have had success with making regular assignments to team members to conduct roll call training for the whole team on an established schedule. The point is that you can get help with an important task. There is plenty of assistance available if you seek it out.

A word of caution: it is often a lot easier to get many cops interested in the "skills" subjects such as firearms and driving than it is in the "softer" topics such as de-escalation techniques and working with special populations. Shooting and driving well certainly are required of the competent police officer, but so are the less-physical skills and abilities. Today more than ever the so-called "soft" skills are expected by the community of the law enforcement practitioner who must function in a society harboring great and sometimes unrealistic expectations of its badge-wearing guardians. You are not serving your people well if you train only in what they enjoy.

Be willing to think outside your comfort zone (or theirs) when you are planning training for your troops. At the same time, the list of the more traditional training topics is virtually without end. Your peoples' needs will, of course, vary somewhat depending upon their assignments and where they do their policing. Detectives will have some training needs that are less critical for patrol officers, and vice-versa. Officers working around a large body of water may require water rescue skills that their colleagues working in an arid environment do not. There is, however, a common core of curriculum topics you can draw upon regardless of duties or locale. Such a list includes at least the following:

Basic first aid
Child neglect and abuse
Neglect and abuse of special
  populations, such as the
  elderly
Crowd control
Mediation and de-escalation
  techniques
Traffic enforcement and
  management
Accident investigation
Computer crime
Observation skills
Courtroom testimony and
  demeanor
Report writing
Warrant preparation and
  service
Police driving
Patrol tactics
Investigative techniques
Interview and interrogation
Officer safety and survival
Traffic stops and vehicle
  searches
High risk vehicle contacts
Local, state, and federal statutes

CPR
Agency policies and
  general orders
Arrest and control tactics
Laws of arrest, search, and
  seizure
Juvenile Code
Evidence recognition and
  collection
Fingerprint and DNA
  evidence
Law enforcement ethics
Radio and computer
  procedures
Dangerous drugs
Managing informants
Use of force laws and
  policies
Structure searches
Community-oriented
  policing and problem-
  solving
Special weapons and tactics
Crime-in-progress response
Legal update
Counter-terrorism response
Crime prevention

Civil situations   Disaster (NIMS) response
Domestic violence intervention   Surveillance techniques

As your team's leader you also will be expected to remain alert for new training needs that result from changes in society and law enforcement. What is the "next big thing?" Whatever it happens to be, if it will affect the way in which you and your employees do your jobs you will need to obtain competent, comprehensive schooling in it.

HOW TO USE A LESSON PLAN

You will have a better chance of getting there with the least amount of trouble if you have a road map of where you are going. This good advice holds true for your training efforts, too. A lesson plan is a kind of map the purpose of which is to identify clearly your destination (goal and objectives) and then provide step by step advice (outline and teaching notes or content) for arriving with a minimum of trouble. A lesson plan will help you as you prepare for a training session, long or short, simple or complex. It will then guide you in conducting it. Planning for an educational endeavor is not greatly different from constructing a plan for the safe capture of a dangerous fugitive. It is needed for both operations.

Lesson plans do not have to be complicated or fancy. They can be typed and placed in a binder or hand-printed on a notepad. They most often include all or some of the following sections:

OVERVIEW OR GOAL. This is a short, general statement describing what it is the training effort is attempting to accomplish. For example: "The officer student will learn how to safely handle a variety of firearms."

OBJECTIVES. Listed here will be the specific skills, abilities, knowledge, or practices that the pupil will be expected to master. The preceding, sample Overview might be followed by these Objectives:

- Objective One: The student will demonstrate safe-handling techniques with the department-issued handgun.
- Objective Two: The student will demonstrate safe-handling techniques with the department-issued shotgun.
- Objective Three: The student will demonstrate safe-handling

techniques with the department-issued rifle.
- Objective Four: The student will demonstrate how to make safe a variety of firearms most likely to be encountered on the job.

OUTLINE/NOTES. This is the material that the instructor will rely on in a presentation to the class. It may be placed in outline form to key the instructor to each topic that he will need to cover. It is a sort of checklist intended to assure that important topics get covered. The instructor may have additional notes that he will use for reference as he talks with and demonstrates to his class of officer-students.

An excerpt from the firearms safety lesson plan outline might look something like this:

I. Safe Handling of the Sig Sauer P226 handgun
  A. Basic Firearms Safety Rules
    1. All firearms are always loaded.
    2. Finger off the trigger until you are ready to fire.
    3. Do not point the weapon at anything you are not willing to destroy.
    4. Be sure of your target and what is beyond it.
  B. Pistol nomenclature
  C. Breakdown of the pistol (demonstration)
  D. Breakdown of the pistol (class participation)
  E. Discussion of accidental discharge incidents and lessons learned
  F. Safe weapon handling techniques (demonstration)
  G. Safe weapon handling techniques (class participation)
  H. Questions and wrap-up

A similar format is employed for the remaining topics covered in the lesson plan.

SOURCES. You as the instructor will include a listing of the resources used to construct the lesson plan. This section serves much the same purpose as the bibliography of a textbook. A reader of the lesson plan is provided with the "authority" behind your presentation. He also is given sources for additional information.

EVALUATION. The final piece of the lesson plan seeks to help you determine if your students mastered the proffered knowledge and skills. Depending on the nature of the material covered, a written test may be the best method for finding out if the student grasps the lesson's contents. Perhaps using the multiple-choice format, the written test may be the best means for checking up on what was learned from a presentation on new statutes. Other subjects, such as arrest and control tactics, might be best tested with individual student demonstrations of the moves that were supposed to have been learned. In the case of the firearms safety lesson depicted here, a combination of written test and practical demonstration might be the best way to go. The multiple-choice test could cover weapon nomenclature and basic safety rules. The hands-on portion of the exam would call for each pupil to demonstrate for the instructor the breakdown and proper handling of each weapon covered in the lesson. For those not obtaining a passing grade remedial training will be required. No one should leave the class still unsure of the subject matter.

Of course, equally important to the student evaluation process will be your observations of your officer-students in the tough classroom of the streets. Are they demonstrating what you worked to teach them? Is further training needed and, if so, for whom? The fact that Patrolman X didn't get it does not necessarily mean that the rest of the group missed it, too. Just like group punishment, group retraining is most often not the right way to go.

The lesson plan can be a big help to you in your training endeavors. It will help you organize your thoughts and information into a logical order for presentation. But do not hesitate to stray from your prepared agenda whenever the in-progress session tells you that you should. The best instructors are flexible in their approach to their teaching task. The questions being asked by your students may tell you that more background information and explanation is needed beyond what you planned in a particular area. Do not be reluctant to take the time to go there. Your class will learn more from the final product. Revise your lesson plan to allow for the additional detail the next time you or another instructor teach from that plan. All lesson plans should be retained and reviewed regularly for needed revisions. As you know, the law enforcement field is a constantly evolving one. Training should change to meet officers' needs.

OVERCOMING TRAINING CHALLENGES

Some leaders seem naturally drawn to a training assignment and truly enjoy imparting knowledge. For others it is a bit more of a challenge. Wherever you fall on this scale there is no doubt that you can and will do an excellent job of preparing your officers for their work. As in so many other areas of life and work, you get better and more comfortable with a task as you gain more experience in doing it. In the process you have the opportunity to discover what works well for you and where you can improve upon your last effort. All of that holds true for training law enforcement employees.

As a leader you must be an advocate for excellent training. Your personal mission should be never to cease adding to your own knowledge of the job. You can then share much of what you learn with your police employees. One of the challenges you will face in a busy law enforcement organization (Which ones *aren't* busy?) is finding time for training amidst all of your team's other responsibilities. Regardless of how much creativity is required on your part, finding the time to train is always worth the effort. You must get it done. You owe it to your people and the law enforcement organization itself which at times may not feel supportive enough of your efforts. When you, your officers, and your agency are sued for real or imagined misconduct, you can bet that "failure to train" will always be one of the allegations levied by a hungry lawyer. You must do your part to assure that such charges are always baseless.

As in so much else you do, being who you are you always will be seeking to get better at what you do. Evaluate your own performance as a teacher. Where do *you* think you could do a better job? Although you will very likely be too hard on yourself you are still the best critic of your own work. But don't stop there. *Ask* some of your students to evaluate your performance. What did they think you did well and where would they like to see improvement? Fixes for some common problems will be self-evident. If the comment is that you talked too fast, concentrate on slowing down. If the session went on for too long, shorten it accordingly. But take all of what you hear with a grain of salt. One veteran law enforcement instructor who gave his students a written evaluation form to complete was amused to find one student commenting that he used "too few videos" while another accused him of using "too many." In the end it is up to you to weigh how much relevance you want to give to student reviews. Nonetheless, they are always worth considering.

In your quest to get better you even can find community college courses and Internet advice to help you become a more skilled teacher. You also can learn much by observing the work of other instructors who are acknowledged to be good at what they do. You just may pick up some "tricks of the trade" you want to employ yourself. You will be paying them a great compliment if you ask permission to observe them in action.

It is perfectly alright to innovate in your approach to law enforcement training. You may come up with something that no one else in your agency has employed before. One leader brought in some minority members of the community to talk with his officers about how they felt about their interactions with police. Some of the cops grumbled at first, but afterwards admitted that they had learned some important points about minority community perceptions as well as actual bias.

Innovation that includes "mixed" approaches to learning can be especially beneficial. Many members of today's generations of employees are not too keen on the "straight lecture" approach to learning. An approach that includes lecture, discussion, questions, and demonstrations of principles covered is likely to have far better results with them. Mixing things up and getting the individual class members involved almost always works well. Don't be hesitant to leave the well-trodden path of instruction. Share your training resources, such as outside speakers and novel techniques, with your peers and expect them to do the same for you. In that way you all can get better. Your agency's employees will be the ultimate beneficiaries.

Don't overlook the possibility that a failure to learn and display increased comprehension of the targeted knowledge or skills may have absolutely nothing to do with your abilities as a trainer. An officer-student may be having difficulty learning because of something going on with him or her, not the instructor. Focus some extra attention on the student who just does not seem to be "getting it." What seems to be the problem? Is he truly challenged in that area or is he simply not interested, whatever the reason? Your observations may need to be followed with some gentle questioning. What does *he* think the problem is? You are not trying to embarrass or accuse him. You are attempting to get across some information that will make his job easier, safer, or otherwise better. You are trying to help.

Don't give up on the slow or resistant learner. Do not permit your training efforts to be deflected by a negative attitude. Remedial training is likely indicated. If your observations tell you that not lack of ability but lack of desire to learn is at the heart of the issue disciplinary action may be indicated to get your point across. It should be clear to the employee that you are not going away.

You have met and handled a lot of challenges in your role as a leader of law enforcement employees. Training challenges should not be an exception to the rule. You must (and will) succeed in your task of trainer.

MEASURING SUCCESS

Your first step in evaluating your success as a trainer is defining what you wanted to see changed in your trainees' job performance. Here you are attempting to measure outcome. Perhaps the training was directed at improving your peoples' accident investigation skills. Success could be measured in the fact that fewer accident reports have to be returned to your officers for additional work. Your observations of their work product would tell you that your efforts have succeeded. But that follow-up observation also could reveal the need for just a bit more work in some particular aspect of the accident investigation process. A supervisory reminder or an additional training session might then be aimed at fixing the remaining shortfall.

Realize that refresher training is required from time to time in many of the knowledge, skill, and ability training areas that peace officers require in order to do their jobs safely and well. The fact that they know or can do something following a training session does not mean that they will retain that talent next year, or six months from now. Repetition will be required. As you know, that is especially true when you are dealing with perishable motor skills, such as arrest and control tactics. Practice may or may not make perfect but it definitely will benefit the learner. Be certain that needed practice does not get overlooked in the daily crush of the job.

Continue to observe your people at work. Identify their new training needs. Continue to ask them periodically where they could use some assistance. Like so much else of what you do as a leader, your job as a trainer is really never done. But with a little extra effort you can measure your success to date and prepare for the next training opportunity. There always will be one.

SUMMARY

You have a number of different tasks to handle in your important role as a trainer of law enforcement personnel. You must first assess your employees' knowledge, skills, and abilities as demonstrated on the job. This will permit you to determine where they are strong and where they may need additional training in order to function safely and effectively as police officers in an increasingly-complex and demanding society. Having determined where they need additional training it is then your responsibility to identify a reliable source for that training. You may utilize others to present it or you may do it yourself. You may rely upon some combination of the two. You also may need to be innovative in how you fit that training into an already full schedule.

You will utilize different modes of training in accomplishing your educational mission. You may rely upon demonstrations, hands-on exercises, video presentations, guest speakers, and mixtures of all of these teaching methods plus others in getting the job done. In the training that you conduct yourself, you will make good use of a lesson plan in setting learning goals and then presenting the necessary information. Then, you will evaluate your peoples' work to determine whether or not the new learning is being displayed in their job performance.

Your own goal has long been never to stop learning your difficult job. You will apply that principle in working with the people who depend upon you to get their own work done well: your officers. They should never reach a point in their careers where learning stops, either. You have a major role to play in assuring that takes place.

For the true professional (that's you) training and its attendant learning are never ending. With your guidance your people will approach their work lives the same way. The excellence they achieve will be a part of your legacy as a great leader.

Chapter 7

CURING THE REPORT-WRITING BLUES

If you are an experienced law enforcement supervisor you likely have come to the same conclusion that many of your peers have reached: too many police officers cannot write very well. This same criticism is heard about this generation's employees from supervisors in all kinds of fields beyond law enforcement. But the lack of written communication ability can prove especially detrimental in a line of work responsible for bringing the dangerous and the guilty to justice. If the criminal case falls apart because of a poorly written police report, a dangerous offender may be released to continue to prey upon the public.

It is neither fair nor accurate to state that police officers as a group cannot write. Many officers do an excellent job of written communication. It is the remaining group that causes serious problems on too many occasions. And that is the group that you, the police supervisor, must address.

Why can't some cops write well? There are probably a number of reasons. But in your efforts to help your people write better it is first necessary to define just what an exceptional police report really is. What needs to be in it? Just as important, what does not belong there? Perhaps most important of all, what can you as these officers' leader do to help poor writers become better scribes? All of these topics are worth further examination.

WHY CAN'T THEY WRITE?

It's not because they are stupid. Law enforcement officers as a group are highly intelligent people. There is no good reason that they cannot *all* develop excellent written communication skills.

But to return to the central question: Why can't they all write well at the outset? Why should a police leader like you have to take the time to teach basic communication skills to a group of smart people? Like the rest of the American population today, these police people face a number of effective communication obstacles. The fact is that there is plenty of blame to go around for this sad state of affairs. You would be joining a long list of supervisors in a wide variety of professions and vocations if you commented that for at least a generation or two the nation's education industry has led youngsters to believe that "ideas are more important than form; it's your thoughts that count." Unless, that is, your organization and spelling and grammar are so poor that the reader has no inkling of what your ideas and thoughts happen to be.

It is no secret that too many educators have lowered their written communication expectations for their students who have now become *your* employees. But has the work world that you inhabit contributed to the problem? The evidence would suggest that it has. Faced with too many employees with too many writing deficiencies, too many employers and their first-line supervisors have surrendered, effectively declaring that the problem is too big to take on. Law enforcement organizations and law enforcement leaders have too often been among them.

In short, in many cases expectations for effective written communication skills have been lowered for the latest generations. Oftentimes, no one has taught these young men and women excellence and demanded it in written form. Leaders have, in too many instances, contributed to the problem through their tolerance of less-than-excellent work. The difficulty has been aggravated by a profusion of handheld communication devices that encourage the use of pop-spelling and sentence fragments: How r u? It is enough to make an old-time grammar teacher weep.

Largely by default you have been given the assignment of helping these people, your subordinates, write better. In doing that, there is an important message you must pass along. Namely, it is this one: You are known throughout the law enforcement organization and beyond by your written work product. If you want to ascend the career ladder, if you seek promotion or that coveted special assignment, you must earn a reputation as an excellent writer. It is the way you get known and respected. It is how you get rewarded. And, by the way, it will keep me, your supervisor, off of your back.

There is no room in police work for lazy or careless writers. Cops can write well. It starts with knowing what belongs (and what doesn't) in a good police report.

WHAT *IS* A GOOD POLICE REPORT?

In every area of their assigned work, your people need to know what you, their boss, expect of them. That rule of thumb holds true for their efforts at report writing. Yes, they were taught in the academy what belongs in a complete police report. But over time shortcuts, both authorized and otherwise, may have inched their way into their report writing. Information they were taught to include sometimes gets left out because with a particular crime or incident it did not feel all *that* important. The report writer cuts corners until corner cutting becomes habit. That's bad for written communication excellence.

It is your job to convince your people to abandon the uncalled-for shortcuts and sloppy writing. That task might be made more difficult because previous supervisors may have not held them so closely accountable. The job needs done nevertheless. It now falls to you to do it.

Many law enforcement agencies dictate the order or format for their officers' reports. They may require events to be reported in chronological order or in some other way. If the police writer abandons the prescribed format, instead wandering and free-lancing his way through the document, he is liable to both confuse and aggravate his readers. It may sound self-evident but experience has demonstrated the need for the advice: stick to the prescribed reporting format. It will make life easier for everyone involved. In this case innovation is better applied to the tactical challenges of the street.

Just what should be contained in that exceptional report? For starters, the basic 5 Ws and an H: who, what, when, where, why, and how. All of the players involved in any way in the action must be clearly identified. That means names are spelled correctly (not guessed at), dates of birth are provided, and addresses are double-checked for accuracy. For that matter, everything that goes into the report must be thoroughly vetted for correctness.

The legal elements of the crime being reported need to be there, too. If an arrest is being reported, probable cause must be carefully laid out for the follow-up investigator or attorney who reads the account somewhere down the road. Remind your officers that their reports must paint a clear picture for the individual who was not there and has no direct knowledge whatsoever of what happened. The report must be detailed and vivid enough that the future reader can see, hear, smell, and feel the scene. That will take some effort but it is worth doing for the added value it will bring in presenting a true picture of events.

In addition to containing correct spelling and grammar, the report should be free of police jargon and strange acronyms and abbreviations. The lay reader is unlikely to know that C.A.T. refers to the Criminal Apprehension Team unless you first spell it out for him.

Police reports should be written in active voice using first person. The witness saw the offender; not the offender was seen by the witness. "I arrested the suspect" is preferable to "the suspect was arrested by reporting officer." Cops don't talk that way; they shouldn't write that way, either. That calls for a first-person narrative.

The language used should be clear, concise, and to the point. Long, complex, convoluted sentences and paragraphs are to be avoided like week-old egg salad. Keep them short. Also, it is important to avoid repeating what has already been said elsewhere in the document. Unnecessary repetition only serves to make the report unnecessarily long and tedious. It is not to the writer's benefit to test the reader's patience.

Remind your officers that they must keep rumors and uncorroborated "facts" out of their police reports. These can be passed along to follow-up investigators, if need be, by other means. Doing so may prevent your officer from later having to explain to an attacking defense attorney why something since established to be untrue nonetheless appears in that officer's official documentation of the incident.

Careful proofreading is a report writer's best friend for producing an excellent product. A careful report writer will first read his or her report for completeness and accuracy. Have all the important elements and details been included? The writer then reads the report a second time, looking for errors of fact, spelling, and grammar. Now is the time to clean up any remaining errors before a critical eye (yours!) examines the finished product. Every good report writer aims for a perfect report that does not have to be returned by the reviewer for additional work. Let your folks know that this state of affairs is what you are seeking, also.

Suggest to your report writers that they put themselves into the reader's shoes. What would they want to know in order to develop a clear understanding of what happened? What would they want to see covered in detail? When their writing has answered those questions to the best of their ability, they probably have completed a good police report. They likewise should know that *you* are going to be that first reader. It is highly probable that if you have unanswered questions after reading it the report is going to be returned to them for more work.

It is hardly fair to expect your officers to write excellent reports without first letting them know what a great report looks like. You must both tell them and show them. You must hold them accountable for the good work that you know they are capable of producing. By doing that early and often you can forestall disappointment for everyone.

HOW CAN YOU HELP THEM?

First and foremost, refuse to accept other than their best work. Do not lower your expectations because one or more of your officers claims to be unable to meet them. You are doing no one a favor if you give in to assertions that "I just can't do it."

There is plenty more you can do to help your report writers even as you hold the line firmly on your expectations for excellence. But do it without ever losing sight of the fact that the responsibility for producing excellent written work belongs first to your employee, not you. That reality must remain clear to the both of you.

Another thing you can do to emphasize the importance of exceptional written communication is to set an excellent example for them in your own written work product. Every good writing tip you provide to your people—the importance of careful proofreading, for example—you also must heed when preparing your own written work. You are seeking to serve as an exceptional role model in this facet of your job as much as you are in any other area, such as officer safety.

The written work you produce is probably most often seen by your employee in the performance review that you complete periodically on him or her. Your admonition to "turn in only your best work" will ring hollow if your own written work contains obvious errors. Write like you (hopefully) drive: with care and not too fast. Proofread painstakingly and repeatedly. Do not allow careless errors to creep into your work. Your employees almost certainly will take note.

That same mandate for only the best work holds true for memorandums, letters, and any other written work you author. Whether you are writing him up for discipline or a commendation your subordinate must witness only your best work. The same requirement applies especially to any police reports you complete as a part of your duties. This sort of writing is, after all, the area in which you are most likely to critique the work of your people. It is absolutely critical that your work is worthy of being copied.

There is something equally important that you can do for your employees to help them become better writers. Provide them with examples of excellent police reports done by other officers. Many of your people are highly visual learners. Looking at a report that you consider complete, accurate, and otherwise well done will help them understand exactly what it is you want from them. Providing copies of these sample reports to your "remedial" writers will give them concrete evidence of precisely what it is you are seeking. One exceptional police supervisor keeps a binder full of particularly well-done police reports, memorandums, warrant affidavits, and letters he can offer his subordinates for help, as needed, in preparing their own written work. Keeping such a resource book likely would be beneficial to you, if you don't already have one. It also would not be a bad idea to suggest to your officers that they keep a similar "scrapbook" of their own. Their own reports that have drawn a supervisor's acclaim belong in there, as well.

Acclaim is a good thing. Do not be stingy with praise when one of your people has done an exceptionally good job of report writing. Reward good writing whenever and however you can. Praise should be deserved but never neglected in report writing as well as in every other area of your employees' job responsibilities. Deserved praise is especially important to a struggling writer who has shown improvement. Encouragement for good work is something virtually everyone appreciates.

Giving individualized help to less-than-great writers is always worth your time. Besides the one-on-one help you can give, there may be formal classes that you can suggest to aid the weak writer. Both community colleges and your employer's Human Resources Department sometimes offer such help. There also may be assistance available on-line through private vendors. Today there is no shortage of competent assistance available to the writer who truly desires to get better.

On a bigger stage you can help strengthen law enforcement officers' writing skills by advocating for those skills to be taught at every opportunity. Let your voice be heard when your department is planning in-service as well as recruit academy training. Do the same if you have a voice at university and community college criminal justice programs in your region. The same holds true for state POST boards. The people who train young officers to write reports need to hear that they could do a much better job of it.

Keep up the pressure for written excellence. Don't overlook your good writers, either. Do not allow any of them to slip into a habit of turning in less than their best written work. Not when they are really busy. Not when they are really tired. Not at all. If it's not up to normal standards—yours, theirs, or both—hand it back. Over the long stretch you will be doing everyone a favor.

Report writers who have improved their work while supervisory focus is on them have been known to slide back into old habits when the spotlight is turned off. Help them by not allowing that to happen. Do not relax your vigilance for doing it the right way.

Good report writing is a team effort. It is the law enforcement officer's responsibility to prepare a police report that is complete and correct in both content and form. It is your task as a leader to require and enforce excellence in that endeavor. When everyone does his or her part the result is a written communication that best serves the interests of justice and the overall public good. As a responsible leader you can take pride in your role in that vital effort.

SUMMARY

Of all the tools he or she must carry around, none is more important to your police officer in carrying out his or her difficult job than the ball point pen and the computer terminal keyboard. It is with these tools that your officer will report his or her observations and fact-gathering for the benefit of a diversity of readers. If the job is not done well, the guilty may escape justice and the citizen deserving of service fail to receive it. Report writing is that important to the law enforcement professional.

There are plenty of contributing factors that help explain why too many of today's cops cannot write well. Rather than assess blame, your primary concern must be to shore up writing skills where they are found wanting. In addition to teaching, this will require you to hand back for revision less-than-good written work. Doing so may not make you popular at the outset, but it is a duty that you must not neglect. Too much is depending upon an excellent police report that paints an accurate picture of what occurred for those who were not there to experience it first-hand. As a consequence you must never lower your expectations for excellent report writing even when you encounter opposition from the writers themselves. It must be clear to your people that you will never accept less than their best work. In the end you will be doing them a favor in addition to benefitting those who must read their written work product.

While in the end the responsibility for producing clear, concise, and informative police reports belongs to the writers themselves, there is plenty you can do to help them. First, you must decline to accept shoddy work. Where necessary, you can point them in the direction of additional schooling. You can provide them with examples of excellent writing. You can set good examples for them through your own written work products. You even can look for ways to reward and commend them when they turn in a consistently excellent written work product.

As a responsible leader it is your duty to advocate for good writing skills in a profession where they have on occasion been neglected. Your people will be better law enforcement officers for the effort. It is one more way in which you as an exceptional leader assure that law enforcement continues to get better all the time.

Chapter 8

EVALUATING EMPLOYEE PERFORMANCE

Performance appraisals, annual reviews, employee evaluations—whatever your organization calls them, for very many people they are about as popular as a fox in a hen house. For too many supervisors, the responsibility to write and deliver these reports is far down on their list of desired things to do. That is probably true for a multitude of reasons. They don't like writing. They have too many other things to do. They think that they have nothing new to say about their employee since the last performance review. They do not want to upset their employee by telling him something he may not want to hear. They don't want their employee not to like them.

Performance reviews and the accompanying one-on-one session with the supervisor are no more popular and probably less so for the employee on the receiving end. This is especially true if the employee already knows that he has had less than a banner year and his supervisor is likely to delve into all of that. Sometimes employees who have reason to expect an overall positive review nonetheless dread the process, even if for no other reason than they do not want to express gratitude for the good words. Cops are, after all, very prideful individuals.

It should come as no surprise then that, particularly in recent years, the cries have gotten louder from employees and supervisors alike to do away with the whole performance review process. A handful of management "experts" has opined that the whole process accomplishes little beyond upsetting people, damaging self-esteem, and instigating employee-supervisor conflict at all levels of the organization.

That's a shame, as there is much good that can come from a properly done and appropriately delivered performance review. The employee can benefit by finding out what he is doing well and where he can improve his performance. The supervisor determines where his employee may need additional work and where the individual's strengths lie. The law enforcement agency sees benefits from an employee who has been commended for his good work and shown where he can do better. The community is the ultimate recipient of sustained or improved performance by a public servant and public service agency.

The law enforcement supervisor really does not have a legitimate reason to dread the performance review process. He should know that an honest performance review can help assure that his employees are performing their vital jobs with maximum effectiveness and efficiency. It helps him do his own job well by telling him where he needs to focus additional attention. And it aids both him and his employee to better serve those paying the freight: the taxpaying citizens.

Any competent supervisor can master the task of writing a comprehensive performance review report and then leading the following sit-down session. This are important parts of his duties. He or she can do this, and do it well. So can you. By utilizing the performance review tips provided in this chapter you can become an exceptional performance review planner, writer, and counselor. It all starts with understanding and communicating to your subordinates why it is important to do it in the first place.

WHY DO IT?

So, if the performance review process is so often dreaded and unpleasant for so many, why do it at all? Concisely put, because a lot of good things can flow from an employee job performance review *properly done*. In other words, it's the right thing to do.

Employees deserve to know how they are doing in the eyes of their supervisor. That supervisor is *you*. The feedback is necessary if they are to alter what they are currently doing in order to meet the expectations of their boss and their organization. An accurate performance review should help an employee get better at his or her job. A well-written work evaluation also assures accountability and assures that an employee is doing what he is supposed to be doing in the manner he is supposed to be doing it. A properly balanced evaluation praises the employee for work well done and focuses his attention where he should do better. The performance review commends good performance and points up where improvement is needed. Finally, an accurate performance review provides evidence and examples to back up necessary personnel actions, both positive and corrective.

You as a leader have an obligation to the employee, his peers, the organization, and the community to help ensure that good work is encouraged and rewarded while areas needing strengthening are identified for corrective action. A police investigator cannot, for example, be justly expected to improve the quality of his reports if he has never been notified that he needs to do so. This advice should have been documented in a well-written and honest performance appraisal.

Most employees want to receive deserved praise from someone they respect. That someone should be you, their supervisor. They can get some of that deserved praise orally. But they also should see it recorded in the performance reviews that you prepare. Most employees also want to know where they can do better. The thorough performance review furnishes that information, too. It is one more way in which you let your subordinates know how they are doing.

An accurate and comprehensive performance review of your police employee benefits you, his or her supervisor. If you intend to either reward or sanction your officer, you will need documentation upon which to base that personnel action. The well-written performance review provides it. If your employee is seeking a special assignment or promotion he likely will want and need your support. That support, where merited, can be furnished through the performance review that you do on this talented employee.

In the end, the entire community benefits from having a more effective, more efficient law enforcement agency with well-prepared people carrying out tasks appropriate for their skill levels. You helped that happen through the act of creating and delivering an accurate performance appraisal. By the same token, you strengthen the police organization and the service it delivers by utilizing the review process to identify employees whose performance must be modified in lieu of removing them from the police service. Of course, that ultimate corrective action still may be necessary if the required improvement in performance does not occur. That is a less pleasant but equally necessary element of your performance appraisal responsibilities. Once more, it is your job and the right thing to do.

Virtually everyone involved benefits in one way or another when you do your job well while serving as a thoughtful evaluator of employee performance. The next question is just how do you go about doing it exceptionally well? It all starts with knowing what not to do.

TRAPS TO AVOID

Throughout your law enforcement career you have discovered that you can learn as much about how to do your job well from your mistakes and the mistakes of others as you can by any other means. That holds true for the preparation and presentation of employee performance reviews. By recognizing these pitfalls you can avoid them in the evaluation reports and performance review meetings that you do. A roster of performance review sins to be avoided includes the following:

Apologize for doing your job. That's the last thing you should do when giving an employee performance review. You undermine the entire process if you do so. You would not apologize to one of your people for giving him a work assignment. Doing a performance review is a work assignment for you, and there is absolutely no reason to be sorry for doing it. Let your employee know that the performance evaluation is an important part of the job for both of you and you see it as such.

Put it off. Procrastinating will not make the job any easier. If you wait until the last possible moment to do it, chances are you will be in a hurry and won't turn in your best work. If you truly don't like doing performance reviews, vow to do them early and get the task out of the way. Then you can concentrate on doing something you consider more pleasurable. In short: Get it done.

Rush through the process. Doing that likely will result in your missing important points in your employee's recent performance. That's not fair to him or her. You seldom do your best at anything when you are in a great hurry. Start early, allow yourself time to think, and give the document time to "cool" before you present it to your employee. You may discover errors or omissions you need to fix. The same holds true for the sit-down session with your employee.

Minimize the whole thing. Telling your employee that the review process is "no big deal" or anything similar to that statement hurts you, the employee, and the organization. The employee has no reason to take what you have to say to heart if you have already indicated that the process is of little or no value. Stress that it is important and will indeed have an impact on his future. If your organization treats the evaluation process as seriously as it should, the statement is valid.

Hand out false praise like candy. Most everyone likes to hear nice things about themselves. Your employees do, too. But giving them plaudits that are not true will destroy your credibility with them. It will not result in them liking you more. Police people are, after all, pretty good at detecting falsehoods. Make sure the nice things you have to say are all true.

Omit significant but unpleasant details. More than a few employee performance reviews done by police supervisors have been handed back to them by their boss for "more work" after their reviewer discovered that a significant misstep or two by the employee being evaluated had been omitted. When that happens, the supervisor involved can lose big points with his or her own boss. The supervisor's courage can even be called into question. An honest work review must contain a summary of all relevant performance, not just the good stuff. Yes, the negative entry may leave the recipient disappointed, even angry. That cannot be helped. It is absolutely necessary that you display the personal courage required to write the whole story, good and bad alike.

Back down if you encounter opposition. On occasion aggressive employees have been known to force their supervisor to take back and revise an evaluation by showing anger or tears upon being confronted with it. Sometimes an employee will do that because he has succeeded in using the tactic with a prior supervisor. You cannot allow that to happen to you. If the employee is able to point out what is clearly an error in the review you certainly should effect the necessary changes. But absent proof that you are mistaken you must stick by your guns. Your reputation for courage and integrity requires no less. Take a break for emotions to cool, if you feel that is advisable. Then finish the session while keeping your own emotions in check.

Permit personal bias to sneak in. The fact that you truly like or dislike an employee you are reporting on should play no part in the performance review you do on him or her. It sounds self-obvious, but it still happens. Report facts, not feelings. You would expect that from your own evaluator. Recognize your feelings, whatever they may be, and be sure that they do not show up in the performance review you conduct.

Compare the review recipient with another employee. The performance review is about one employee and no one else. Never compare his or her performance with that of another employee, no matter how much you might wish the two could be similar. "You need to be more like Samantha" almost certainly will lead to a total disruption in your supervisory relations with Bobbi Jo. Do not do it. Not ever.

Use the last one to write the next one. It may happen more often than you think. A supervisor, pressed for time or just plain lazy, retrieves the last performance review on Employee X, changes the dates and a few words here and there, and turns it in as the new one. The excuse is, of course, "he hasn't done anything differently from last time." The truth is he has *always* done something differently from last time. He deserves to have it noted, good, bad, or otherwise. Do not be guilty of that sort of subterfuge.

Skip it if no one is looking. It has happened more than once or twice that a responsible supervisor goes looking for his employee's last evaluation only to find there isn't one on file, perhaps for years. The organization itself is as guilty as its neglectful supervisors if this travesty is allowed to happen. The employee, the supervisor, and the employee himself all need to know how he is doing. That cannot happen effectively if no one is recording his performance. If your agency has a performance review system, assure that you do not fail to complete the required performance review on time. It is one of your tasks as a leader.

All of these are, of course, failed responses to the performance review challenge. They are prime examples of how *not* to write a performance review or conduct a performance review meeting. But that being the case, how *should* the task be accomplished? That discussion comes next.

HOW TO DO IT WELL

You can do this and do it well. You have mastered the other writing assignments of your job and you can master this one, too. That holds true even if doing performance reviews will never be your favorite thing to do. By setting yourself to do it, reserving time for the process, and staying on task you can complete a job that will benefit the employee and the organization. You then can move on to the other things that are awaiting your attention, secure in the knowledge that you have you ably have taken care of yet another of your important responsibilities.

Naturally, in assembling the review document you will utilize the forms and formats dictated by your agency. Some organizations rely on rating by numbers, such as 1 through 5 with the highest number reserved for exceptional performance. Others use descriptive labels for performance, such as "Superior" or "Needs Improvement." Many require narrative, as well. All of them should. Whatever the case, follow your employer's evaluation preparation guidelines. You do not need to have it kicked back by HR after you have put a lot of time and effort into the task.

Just which aspects of your employee's performance are to be evaluated? Again, the tasks and responsibilities and expectations will vary at least somewhat from one place to the next. Nevertheless, a certain core of talents and traits most often reviewed includes the following components:

Job knowledge	Professional appearance
Technical skills	Teamwork
Officer safety	Attendance and punctuality
Firearms proficiency	Tact, patience, restraint
Driving skills	Overall quantity of work
Customer service	Overall quality of work
Communication (written and oral)	Acceptance of supervision
Decision-making and judgment	Leadership
Geography of the jurisdiction	

There likely will be other performance elements depending on the type and locale of law enforcement organization employing you and your subordinate. Oftentimes the review format permits you, the supervisor, the leeway to add additional elements particular to the employee's specific responsibilities. You should fully utilize that feature if you feel it will enable you to more accurately describe your subordinate's work.

The performance review process can be divided into two parts: preparation of the review document and the one-on-one session in which it is presented to and discussed with the police employee. Here are some experience-proven tips for successfully carrying out both tasks:

Preparing the Review

RESERVE ENOUGH TIME TO DO IT RIGHT. You do not want to rush through the evaluation writing assignment. The quality of your work likely will drop if you speed through it. Avoid the busiest times of your day, which for many supervisors occur at the beginning and end of the shift. Formally schedule yourself a block of time and then stick to your agenda. You may need to set aside time on several days to do it correctly without rushing.

DON'T SPRING ANY SURPRISES. Your employee should not be seeing something negative for the first time when he reads his evaluation. You should have advised him well in advance about what you perceived as performance in need of repair. Surprises at performance review time tend to spur anger and result in unnecessary conflict. Even if (or especially if) there is less-than-great news ahead, let the recipient know that it is coming so that he has an opportunity to try to fix his performance if he is of a mind to. If he succeeds in doing so, that needs review comment, too.

PROVIDE EVIDENCE FOR YOUR ASSERTIONS. Specific examples of the performance you are commenting on strengthen your position and the review itself. It is not enough to state that your employee is "sometimes discourteous with citizens." You must cite specific instances of when this has happened. In doing so you are establishing a sort of "probable cause" for the opinions you are putting forward in the performance review. Do not neglect to provide backing for whatever it is you have to say, positive or less so.

STAY FOCUSED. As you begin thinking about your employee's work it may be all too easy to start down a sidetrack regarding some incident or observation that really doesn't bear on his current performance. Be careful not to wander astray as you prepare the document. His current marital difficulties, for example, are not appropriate fodder for a work performance evaluation. Keep your comments focused on the topics covered by the performance review.

DO NOT TAKE SHORTCUTS FOR SENIOR OR HIGHLY SUCCESSFUL EMPLOYEES. It may be tempting to skip some categories or details when you are writing about a clearly successful or very senior employee, the former because you feel there is little he can do to improve and the latter because you don't think he will change, anyhow. That's not fair to either employee. Give each the complete review he merits.

DISPLAY COURAGE AND TELL THE TRUTH. It is important enough to state again: Do not minimize bad behavior or omit significant happenings from the evaluation period because you are concerned that the employee will be upset at seeing them in writing. Be up front with your subordinate in reporting on the not-as-good along with the good. It is your job as an ethical leader. If there are things to be recorded that will upset your employee, it's worth remembering that they are present as a consequence of his doing, not yours. Your own supervisor will not be favorably impressed if he fails to see noted significant behavior that he is aware of and expected to see covered in your report.

REPORT ON THE ACCOMPLISHMENT (OR NOT) OF PREVIOUSLY ESTABLISHED GOALS. Sometimes employees have goals and objectives established in their last performance review but never see a comment in the subsequent review as to whether or not those targets were achieved. The performance review loses some of its value if that is allowed to happen. Carefully review the prior evaluation for goals (there *should* be some) and then record whether or not they were met. If not, note why that happened and if they are to be renewed for the upcoming evaluation period.

SET GOALS FOR THE NEXT EVALUATION PERIOD. Clearly describe for your subordinate what it is you want to see accomplished during the upcoming review period. Ask him ahead of time if there are personal goals he would like to see included. There is no specific number of goals or objectives that should be established. If it is a difficult or complex one, a single goal may be plenty. (Example: Improve the quality of your written reports and affidavits.) Otherwise, two to four should suffice.

FACTOR IN THE AGENCY'S MISSION AND GOALS, WHERE FEASIBLE. Your agency may have its own, department-wide goals. If that is the case, try to tie one or more of your employee's performance review goals into that bigger picture. For example, if your department has a goal of "improving traffic safety" it may be appropriate to give your nightwatch officer the performance review goal of increasing his drunk driving enforcement efforts.

BE CONSCIOUS OF THE "HORNS OR HALO" EFFECT. Few employees are totally messed up or absolutely perfect. Evidence and examples of performance, good or bad, are important and must be included in the review document. But even a really challenging employee may have done *something* well. Include that, too. And if an exceptional employee has nevertheless committed a significant "uh-oh" that reality should not be ignored just because he's normally a solid performer.

LOOK PAST YESTERDAY. It is natural to write about things that are fresh in your memory. But it is possible that significant events in your employee's performance happened many months ago but were still within the current evaluation period. If you keep notes informally or in a supervisor's logbook you are more likely to recall these things for mention now. Consider keeping such a record, even if your employer does not require it. It will make preparing the performance review document a lot easier as well as more complete. If you are doing an *annual* review it should not be limited to the last two months of performance. Be sure to cover events of the entire review period.

DOUBLE-CHECK YOUR WORK FOR ACCURACY. Your employee needs to know that the performance review process is a Big Deal to you, his supervisor. He is unlikely to believe that if the thing is sloppily done. Proofread your evaluation report for both content and form. Be sure you have got your facts straight and your spelling correct. Then proofread it again.

Presenting the Review

After a lot of thought and effort you have the completed document in hand. You have done a good job, but your work is still only halfway completed. Now you must sit down with your employee and present the results of your work—and his. Here are a few suggestions that have worked for other leaders in making the session a productive one:

PICK THE RIGHT TIME AND PLACE TO DO IT. The right time to conduct the performance review meeting is *not* when you or your employee are rushed and thinking about the other tasks you must get done in a limited amount of time. Your meeting place should be calm, quiet, and totally away from chattering radios and jangling cell phones. (Those devices should not even be present, if at all possible.) The meeting does not have to take place in an office or interview room. If there is a quiet corner booth at the coffee shop that venue might even suffice. How much privacy you will require may depend on what you have to say and what you expect the employee's reaction to be. If your judgment tells you a very private location is required, arrange for it. But be sure the session is not rushed to completion. The employee must have every opportunity to ask questions and make his own comments. You will need plenty of time to respond. No time limits should be placed on the meeting.

ALLOW THE EMPLOYEE TO PREVIEW THE DOCUMENT. Your employee should have at least hours, not minutes, to look over the evaluation ahead of the meeting. This will allow him to form any questions he might have about what you have to say. He also should have time to pull together any documentation he may want you to see that he believes may prove something contrary to your assessment. The purpose of the preview is not to undermine your work but to assure that the employee concludes that he has had a fair hearing of any differences. In actuality, giving the employee time to review your work is unlikely to lead to serious differences of opinion in most cases.

BE EMPATHETIC BUT TELL THE TRUTH. You should be tactful in what you have to say, pro or con, about your employee's performance. Your tone should never be hostile or accusatory. This sit-down is not supposed to be a "gotcha" session. But do tell the truth. If he needs to make drastic improvements in his report writing, don't say that "some minor tweaks" are needed. Let him know up front that major improvement is required to avoid formal corrective action, if that is indeed the case. Most cops appreciate a straightforward, no-nonsense approach by their supervisor. Empathy is appropriate; minimizing the impact of substandard performance is not.

BE PREPARED TO BACK UP YOUR STATEMENTS. Now is the time to present the examples and evidence that substantiates what you have to say, good or bad. Clear documentation of performance often has the effect of eliminating or minimizing arguments from the evaluation recipient. Be certain that the instances you cite actually occurred and that you are reporting them accurately. Then, lay out the evidence for your employee to examine. Once again, you are not trying to come across as accusatory. You are just calmly reporting on past performance by providing examples of what you are talking about.

STAY ON THE SUBJECT AT HAND. The two of you are present to discuss the performance review on the table, not events and people from years past. The fact that your employee did not feel her last supervisor was a nice person probably has little relevancy to the current discussion. Neither does her performance five years ago, positive or negative. Don't permit your subordinate to lead you down rabbit trails that distract from the purpose of the meeting. Bring him or her back to the purpose of the meeting. You can discuss those "other issues" later, if he or she wishes. But stay on task, and the task of the moment is an employee performance review.

OWN YOUR WORK. Demonstrate your personal courage by taking responsibility for what you have written and said about your employee. Do not blame a negative comment in the review on what someone else allegedly has said. This is your work product, not the chief's, not the captain's. You will need the courage to look your subordinate in the eyes and reinforce what you have to say, positive or negative. This is not the time to stare at the clock on the wall or examine your shoes. Call upon the courage that you have aplenty.

BE PREPARED FOR EMOTIONAL DISPLAYS AND DIS-AGREEMENT. Don't be fearful if you anticipate resistance from an employee during the performance review sit down, but do steel yourself for tears or angry displays if you expect those, perhaps based on previous behavior of the employee. Employees have on occasion been known to utilize those tactics to back down a supervisor. Be patient, be empathetic, be considerate, but go ahead with what you had planned to say. Say something positive, if it's appropriate, but do not get distracted from the purpose of the meeting: a review of a subordinate's performance.

TAKE A BREAK, IF NECESSARY. You do not want to get into a back and forth, "yes you did, no I didn't" circular argument with your employee. That will not accomplish anything good. If you sense that rhetoric is getting heated, perhaps on both sides, call a break for emotions to cool. But the break should be for minutes, not days. An employee should not be allowed to derail the performance review effort through dramatics, even if they are quite sincere. Make an extra effort to remain calm when the session resumes, whether the employee is or not.

BE CERTAIN ANY DOCUMENT CHANGES YOU MAKE ARE WARRANTED. You should not alter the performance review document just because its recipient disagrees with something it contains. If it is simply a choice of words that the two of you are at loggerheads over, it's up to you to decide if you want to make a change in word selection. If doing so will cool emotions it may be worth doing. But changes in reported facts and conclusions should not be made without proof from your employee that the report as written is in error. The document is, after all, your written work product, not the employee's.

SET GOALS FOR THE NEXT EVALUATION PERIOD. A thorough performance review should set targets for the employee to accomplish during the upcoming review period. Even if your agency does not require the inclusion of goals and objectives, it is a good idea to give your employee something to work towards. You can and should ask for the employee's help in establishing these targets. But proceed with setting them even if he or she has nothing particular in mind. The goals, of course, should be worthwhile and require some actual effort but not be practically unreachable.

CONCLUDE WITH A SUMMARY–POSITIVE, IF FEASIBLE. It is helpful to you, the employee, and any other reader if you close the performance review with a short summary of the document. This should be done both in writing and orally. If there are commendable highlights in the employee's performance (there almost always will be *something*), be sure to mention it. While it probably cannot happen every single time that you conduct a performance review session, it is always preferable to leave your employee with the feeling that the meeting was worthwhile and not something to be dreaded in the future.

ALERT YOUR BOSS IF YOU ANTICIPATE PROBLEMS. On rare occasions an employee may be dissatisfied enough with your review that he or she wants to appeal it to the next level of the chain of command. That is the employee's right in most organizations. Just be sure you make your boss aware of the situation in advance. Let him or her know the basis for the performance review statements as well as the employee's apparent beefs. Be prepared to answer questions concerning how you reached your evaluation conclusions. There is no need to be apologetic, resentful, or angry about having to explain your work. If you have done it well, you have nothing to be concerned about. Your employee is exercising his or her rights and you are doing the job you are paid to do.

The objective is that you and your employee reach the conclusion of the performance review session each with the feeling that something positive and useful has been accomplished. That is unlikely to be the case with every single review you ever conduct. Regardless, your responsibility remains to be fair, tell the truth, and do your best to get the honest message across. If any bad feelings remain, they should not come from you, the ethical, empathetic, but honest evaluator. Know that you have done the job that you promised to do to the best of your ability when you accepted the invitation to leadership's ranks.

THE FOLLOW-UP

A performance review accomplishes little good if the document is filed away never to be seen again and the accompanying presentation session promptly forgotten by all parties once it is completed. But too often that is what is permitted by a reviewer relieved to be "finished" with the whole process. As a responsible supervisor you will not allow that to happen.

When you pick up an employee from a previous supervisor one of your first tasks should be to review your new subordinate's most recent performance review, assuming there is one. (There should be.) This you do in addition to discussing that employee's performance with his previous boss. Let your employee know that you have done this—there should be nothing secretive about it. Make him or her aware that you have noted any strengths as well as "needs improvement" areas highlighted by the previous supervisor. In fairness, the employee needs to be on notice that you will be following up on any areas where additional work is needed. Then, do what you promised.

Follow-up also is required for the performance reviews that you author. Without hovering, check up on the progress (or lack of same) that your subordinate is making in the called-for areas. Be honest with him or her. Acknowledge and commend progress where you find it. Also bring to the employee's attention any area in which you do not see needed change in job performance taking place. Reiterate what it is you need and expect to see. You owe that frank discussion to both the employee and the organization.

Take notes (document!) on the change or lack of change that you observe so that you can report on it in the next performance review that you will complete on that subordinate. Let him or her know that you are doing so. Once more, there should be no secrets involved with the performance review process.

Never hesitate to confront "slippage" in an employee's job performance that has previously been rated as exceptional or acceptable. Perhaps Officer Bob's courtesy and demeanor drew high marks in his most recent performance review. But since then he has incurred multiple citizen complaints for discourtesy. Something is going on. Document confirmed problems. Talk with Officer Bob to find out what is happening. Let him know that improvement is both needed and expected. Be prepared to cover the problem and the results in his next performance review. Know that you have done the right thing and carried out another of your most important responsibilities as a good leader. And again: never apologize for doing your job. If disciplinary action must be imposed for an employee who, absent a valid explanation, has failed to carry out a performance review's requirements, that is the employee's doing, not yours. Know that you have done your job as an ethical leader.

If the employee whose performance you have recently reviewed is moving on to a new supervisor, make the effort to brief his or her new boss on relevant issues contained in that review. If that supervisor is doing his job well, he will want the information. It's your job to present it. If your review of the employee calls for some kind of follow-up action, his new supervisor needs to be aware of it if the individual is to be held appropriately accountable.

It is all too easy to "file it and forget it" once the performance review process feels completed. But it hasn't been completed until the necessary follow-up has been done. Persistence and courage alike are required to finish the job. Both of those qualities you have in ample supply. You will complete an important if difficult task. That's the kind of leader you are.

SUMMARY

You, unlike some of your peers, do not dread conducting a performance review of a police employee. That is true because you realize the good for the employee, the supervisor, the law enforcement organization, and the community that can come from such a review done the right way. You recognize that when the document is prepared correctly and administered appropriately the efficiency, effectiveness, and overall performance of both the employee and the organization are improved. In the final analysis, the overall well-being of the employee can benefit, too.

A performance review done well assures accountability, helps an employee become stronger, addresses performance weaknesses, and recognizes work well done. It gives the police employee the supervisory feedback he or she deserves. It provides evidence for needed personnel actions, either positive or corrective in nature. It strengthens the law enforcement organization, one employee at a time.

Doing a performance review well requires that you avoid apologizing for doing your job. It requires being totally honest with the review recipient. It requires that you avoid putting off the task as an "unpleasant" but necessary duty and then rushing through it when you can no longer procrastinate. It requires that you steer clear of false accolades but also avoid unfair and baseless criticism. In a few words, the entire review process demands both honesty and courage on your part.

Doing it the right way also mandates that you write thoughtfully and carefully and then proofread your work for both form and content. You fully understand that if the employee is to take the whole process as the important matter it is he or she must see evidence that you, too, realize its importance as seen in the effort you have put into it. You also recognize that you must tell the truth always but show empathy and understanding as required. You remain focused, avoid rabbit trails and side issues, and set goals and objectives for expected employee performance going forward. You also follow-up performance reviews, where necessary, to assure that called-for progress is being made. You do not seek to come across as heavy-handed or unfeeling in the performance review meeting, but neither do you back down in the face of unmerited opposition.

Carrying out fair, honest, and comprehensive employee performance reviews is a required and important task for the law enforcement leader. You can do it and do it well sans the dread that too often seems to accompany that responsibility. You can do it well because of the kind of solid and courageous leader that you are.

Chapter 9

YOUR RESPONSIBILITIES FOR OFFICER
SAFETY AND RISK MANAGEMENT

You have a great many responsibilities as a law enforcement leader. None is more important than doing your best to help your people stay safe on the job. You likewise have risk manager responsibilities that require you to monitor your officers' work for conduct that could expose them and the organization to unnecessary legal liability. After all, career and financial survival are parts of officer survival, too. Your responsibilities require that you intervene, for example, when one of your charges pilots his patrol car like a race car down a crowded residential street. You realize that such conduct cannot be allowed to become his "standard" behavior.

You serve as a sort of safety officer for your department. You are responsible for monitoring and inspecting the actions and attitudes of your troops to assure that they are laboring safely in a field full of risks. You are responsible for providing additional training for your people when you detect officer safety lapses or become aware of new or changed threats to their welfare. You additionally are required to advocate for your people for needed safety equipment or changes in tactics and procedures. And you are required to speak up for your employees when they have done it the right way for safety but are questioned or criticized for their actions. Indeed, you have a lot to do when it comes to officer safety, survival, and risk management.

Before you can do the rest of your job well you need to know where some of the dangers to you and your people lie. The vital task of identifying those dangers will be covered next.

WHERE LIES THE DANGER?

There was a day when a police recruit's training included virtually nothing titled "officer safety and survival." That is no longer the case and it has not been for quite some time. Nevertheless, on occasion, because it is hot, or cold, or raining, or it is late in the shift, or for a dozen other "reasons" a peace officer cuts corners and neglects to employ what he has been taught about staying safe on the street. If he is lucky, he gets away with it. Nothing bad happens. And because nothing bad happens this time, unsafe behavior becomes ingrained as a habit—a bad habit that can kill.

It is your job to seek out those unsafe practices and bad habits where they exist and see to it that they are eliminated. You do that by spending plenty of time in the field to inspect your officers' safety-related performance. There is not a shortcut to getting it done properly. Your eyes-on observation is required. But what, exactly, are you looking for even while hoping not to see it?

The safety errors that have contributed to the death or injury of thousands of law enforcement officers over many years have changed very little ever since there has been something called law enforcement. The weapons and other threats have changed somewhat; the safety mistakes have not. The potentially fatal errors law enforcement officers too often make include at least the following:

Complacency, apathy, general carelessness. An officer who "just doesn't care," who sleepwalks his way through his job, or does it in a sloppy, careless manner is setting himself up for a hard fall, perhaps a fatal one. Sometimes such an officer simply doesn't think anything bad could happen to him, other times he doesn't feel whatever he does will matter, anyway. He's mistaken. This officer is a danger to his peers. His complacency and carelessness may be catching to others. Many other officer safety errors may accompany this one.

Making dangerous assumptions. Anything not known for certain must be considered an assumption. An officer may make a fatal mistake by assuming all alarms are false. They aren't. He may assume that an offender will not fight him because he didn't fight during his last five arrests. But this time he might. A law enforcement officer safely can make very few assumptions beyond the one that says any situation or individual can hold danger for him or her.

False courage. Sometimes this is referred to as Tombstone Courage. It is exemplified by this statement: "I don't need a backup." This officer may be trying to prove that he's not afraid. He may be trying to convince others of his bravery. He may be trying to convince himself. Whatever the case, this critical error has resulted in the deaths of countless officers over the years.

Failing to detect and react to the danger signs. There are a number of danger signs that should tell the observant officer that danger may be lurking just around the corner. A simple example may be found in the suspicious individual who is keeping one or both of his hands out of sight—because he is holding a weapon. The officer who misses this danger sign or, just as bad, detects it but bulldozes ahead with no change in his tactics is setting himself up for tragedy. It is known that many officer deaths have followed just this scenario: the danger signs have been evident but missed or ignored moments before tragedy occurred.

Underestimating an opponent. Some violent criminals are just as good at their "trade" as the officer is at his. Some are physically fit—perhaps more fit than the officer they are going up against. Some are very familiar with weapons and are competent with them. The "sloppy drunk" may still be plenty scrappy. The emotionally disturbed man may seem to have superhuman strength. Not being ready to face such a challenge could prove fatal to the unprepared officer.

Improper use of backup help. Failing to call for necessary assistance could prove fatal. But so could having plenty of help on hand but not using it wisely. Backup help that is standing around shooting the breeze is of little help and may, in fact, increase the danger factor for everyone. The officer fortunate enough to have backup must use it wisely.

Failure to watch the hands. Biting and kicking aside, it is a suspect's hands or the weapon he puts in them that are most likely to be responsible for the death or injury of a law enforcement officer. If an officer cannot see both of a suspect's hands at all times that in itself should be considered a sign of potential danger. An individual may have his hands in his pockets because it's cold outside or that may simply be his chosen posture. But until the officer establishes that fact for certain he faces the potential for added risk from hands he cannot see.

Careless approach or positioning. Allowing a subject to stand too close to him is an example of this officer safety error. So is standing directly in front of a door he is knocking at on a call. So is standing between the front bumper of his patrol car and the rear bumper of a traffic violator's vehicle—that's a great place to get crushed between the vehicles. An officer allowing a prisoner to walk behind him is committing another potentially terminal error. And so is moving in too close too soon at the end of a confrontation with an offender.

Poor weapon retention practices. Every call or contact a police officer engages in contains one or more firearms—his own. If he is not very cautious they could end up in the hands of an enemy. Virtually every year in the United States one or more law enforcement officers are shot to death with their own firearm.

Failure to wear or use protective equipment. There is no valid reason for a law enforcement officer not to be wearing body armor when he is working the street. There is no valid excuse for not wearing his lap and shoulder belts in a moving vehicle. Yet every year officers perish because they were not using these simple protective tools. The loss of life is both tragic and needless.

Poor use of cover. Regularly officers die from an offender's bullets even though what would have amounted to good protective cover was close by. Sometimes officers are killed after leaving excellent cover. In yet other instances cops confuse cover with concealment and are fatally wounded after sheltering behind something that can be pierced by an offender's bullets.

Poor handcuffing practices. Sometimes bad things happen to officers because they applied the cuffs too tightly or too loosely. Sometimes terrible things happen because a cop fails to double-lock these temporary, fallible restraint devices. On occasion peace officers die because they cuffed a subject in front of his body rather than behind. And, believe it or not, other times they perish violently because they failed to handcuff an arrestee at all.

Poor searching practices. Sometimes officers die because they failed to search a prisoner thoroughly. (A poor search may be even worse than none at all because of the false sense of security it may leave.) Other times they are killed because they did not repeat their search a sufficient number of times. And, yes, they sometimes die because they omitted the needed search completely. It is seemingly unbelievable but all too true.

Failure to look for the next threat. The bad guy who has just been captured may not be the only offender hiding in the building. The knife your officer just retrieved from the arrestee's clothing may not be the only weapon he is hiding. Prematurely ceasing the search for threats—human or otherwise—has contributed to far too many law enforcement casualties.

Relaxing too soon. Officers have relaxed their vigilance once a suspect is in handcuffs, or in the back of the patrol car, or within the confines of the police station only to be injured or killed by a still-dangerous offender. Officers also have been slain while enjoying a coffee or meal break in the local restaurant. You must stress to your troops the need to maintain constant vigilance on the job.

Being sleepy, asleep, or sick on the job. If an officer is not at his best he should not be on duty. One officer was murdered by a passing felon after falling asleep while doing a report in her patrol car. Anything that distracts an officer from his focus on survival makes him more susceptible to injury, whether from an offender or an accident. Distractions include both sleepiness and illness.

Poor prisoner handling practices. Some misguided officers think the danger is gone or minimized once an offender is in custody. If that were true law enforcement would not have lost the number of officers it has to already-in-custody offenders. Officers also have been murdered by their colleagues' carelessly-handled prisoners. Offenders remain potentially dangerous whether in custody or otherwise.

Being out of shape physically or mentally. On occasion cops have died because they gave up the fight after being injured. Others have perished because they were out of shape or otherwise not as fit as the offender they had gone up against. Your people must be at the top of their game in all respects if they are to survive the sometimes-mean streets.

Failure to comprehend the danger of accidents. Most years as many cops die in accidents as are murdered by violent criminals. Vehicle accidents are the most common cause of accidental deaths of law enforcement officers. Your people need to know that. They also need to understand the need to use caution in all their on-the-job activities, not just when they are matching wits with criminals.

Failure to learn from experience. Experiences, good and bad, can be the most effective teachers. If your subordinates are not examining their previous adventures and misadventures on-duty they are missing great learning opportunities. They cannot be permitted to do that. Critiquing their own safety performance, perhaps with your help, will make your people safer.

Of all the safety errors that law enforcement officers make, the attitude of complacency and general carelessness is likely the deadliest of all. It is the umbrella under which many other officer survival errors gather. If you don't think anything bad can happen to you or if you believe nothing you do can forestall an event "destined" to occur you are apt to be guilty of a lot of officer safety lapses. Combatting this defeatist attitude wherever you find it in yourself or among your people has to be your highest priority. You must get across to your troops that everything they do does matter. They need to know that they literally can save their own lives. As in so many other areas of life, a positive attitude is everything. A winning, "I will survive no matter what" mindset is what you are seeking to establish in each of your officers as well as yourself.

You should remain aware that while law enforcement officers and law enforcement training focus on the dangers posed by human hazards likely to be encountered on the job, cops continue to be hurt or killed in comparable numbers in accidents of all kinds. That's where your role as a risk manager comes into play. It is up to you to assure that your people don their body armor, wear their seat belts, drive at safe speeds in both routine and emergency responses, and handle all of their deadly weapons with the utmost caution. You will show them the video clips and news stories from elsewhere showing their peers who have done things the wrong (or right) way. As you know, there is much to be learned from the actions of others, good or bad.

As you review the fatal errors that law enforcement officers sometimes make you will recognize that there is no such thing as a "routine" traffic stop or a "simple" arrest. You will acknowledge that potentially deadly errors are made by rookies and veterans alike. You are well aware that a novice officer intent on doing everything right may actually be more safety-smart than the old salt who thinks he has seen everything and is lax in his safety practices. You realize that unsafe behavior must be corrected whether it is committed by the green-as-grass youngster or the grizzled old salt. You know that "really good cops" make mistakes, too. They need your attention, also.

Officers do not hit the street with the intent of being killed or maimed by a violent offender. You should never lose sight of the fact that vicious criminals are responsible for the carnage. But by setting himself up for harm by neglecting basic officer safety practices the careless officer makes it much easier for the criminal successfully to attack him. You have a key role to play in preventing that from happening. But how do you do it?

INSPECTING FOR SAFETY

There are readily apparent things you can do in the interest of officer safety. You can inspect your people, formally in a line-up or informally, one at a time, to see that their weapons and other protective equipment are well-maintained and functional. You can watch to assure that they are adhering to their employer's rules regarding the wearing of body armor and the consistent use of the lap and shoulder belts in their vehicles. You can observe to be sure that they are handling their weapons and their police vehicle in a safe manner. All of these things you are obliged to do, but you can and must do more.

You should be closely attentive to the practices and tactics your people use on the street. If you observe that an officer's prisoner searching technique could use improvement, you address it. If you note that your investigator is traipsing about the station unarmed, you deal with that, too. (You might want to remind him that more than one or two cops have been murdered within the walls of their own building.)

You must inspect more than equipment and practices. Safety *attitudes* need inspected, as well. You know from experience that young officers can make critical safety errors based upon both lack of experience and a desire to prove themselves in front of their peers. Your teaching can help solve the lack of knowledge problem. But a no-nonsense sit-down with you may be required to disabuse them of their Tombstone Courage approach to their job. That attitude cannot be tolerated and they must hear just that from you, their boss.

On the other hand, you may have a very senior employee who thinks he has seen everything, done everything, and has no time for that silly officer safety nonsense. This may be the same individual who believes that "whatever will happen will happen regardless of what I do." This misguided and fatalistic attitude must be fixed before it infects the other members of your team. He can believe whatever he wants but for the safety of his colleagues he cannot be permitted to display his beliefs in his on-the-job behavior. Granted, he may pose a greater counseling challenge than does his green peers. But you are up to the task. The job must be done right away. Good officer survival practices demand no less.

A comprehensive safety inspection likewise should include your taking a look at your own safety perspective. Are your attitudes and practices what you want your people to see and copy? Are you truly setting a good example? More about that later.

MAKING YOUR PEOPLE SAFER

You already know about the officer safety errors that can endanger your people. You realize the importance of inspecting for safe job performance. You know how important it is that your officers do their jobs in the right (translate that to mean the *safe*) way. But exactly what is it that you need to reinforce with your troops as you work to help them survive their too-often hazardous job? Some of the safety directives you must enforce include these:

Never become complacent. You have never seen it all or done it all. You know that. You must be sure your troops know it, too. Complacency and general carelessness already have killed enough law enforcement officers; so has apathy. Do not allow any of your people to add to the total.

Keep learning your job always. You never know it all. Neither do your subordinates. Encourage your officers to further their law enforcement safety training at every opportunity. Critique their critical incident experiences with them to assure that they learn as much as possible from the encounters. That is another way you help them avoid deadly complacency.

Maintain a winning mindset. You know that some horribly wounded colleagues of yours have survived only because they determined not to allow a violent criminal to beat them. Make your officers aware of some of these incidents. Stress to them the importance of never giving up but instead fighting through to victory over a would-be cop killer.

Don't work at becoming a hero. Throughout a long law enforcement career a man or woman stands a good chance of doing something lifesaving and heroic, probably on more than one occasion. There is no reason to force such a situation into being. Taking ridiculous chances without good cause and without help has led to the death of more than one law enforcement officer. You must counsel your troops against actively seeking hero status.

Always keep looking for one more. One more suspect, one more weapon, one more threat. If your cops find an offender hiding in a building, they must secure him and begin searching for the next one, whether he is known to exist or not. When they find him he is secured in turn and the search resumed. Your people should never abandon their threat awareness.

Listen to the little voice. It is likely that it is your common sense that is voicing itself, and if a cop is wise he or she will pay attention. Made up of both training and life experience, the little voice of common sense is, for example, telling your officer not to walk up to the car he has just pulled over. Something just does not feel right. He needs to hang back behind cover and wait for assistance. If nothing bad happens, all the better. But the application of good common sense may have prevented a tragedy.

Maintain a "reactionary gap." Observe to make sure your officers maintain a distance of at least five to six feet from subjects they are dealing with on the street. Circumstances, such as an obviously hostile subject, may dictate increasing the distance. Your officer needs the time to move and react with appropriate tactics if the individual launches a sudden attack. He is less likely to counter a surprise attack successfully if he has allowed the subject to be too close.

Use your help wisely. An officer's backup must understand what it is the primary officer wants him to do, and how. This requires practice and excellent communication. It's called contact and cover and it works to prevent unnecessary injuries and deaths. The contact or primary officer conducts the main business of the contact (arrest, searching, ticket writing, etc.) while the cover serves as a lifeguard, prepared to intervene instantly if the contact officer is menaced by a threat from anyone or any quarter. Backups must never be allowed to lounge around gassing with one another. Watch for this like a hawk and intervene if you spot such behavior. Backup help is too precious to waste.

Think cover. An officer has a lot to think about while handling in safety all the human contacts he makes on the job. But you must encourage him to reserve at least a piece of his brain to think about where he can go quickly for cover in case a weapon suddenly appears. Virtually any cover is better than standing in the open engaging in a gunfight with a criminal. Cover consciousness should be a part of a safety-savvy officer's thought processes whenever he is on the job.

Handcuff and search properly. Both skills are learned not from a book or a video presentation but from regular hands-on practice under the supervision of a competent instructor. You also need to remind your people that the searching process is at least a bit safer if it follows, not precedes, the handcuffing process. Poor handcuffing or searching practices are not malpractices you can tolerate from your charges. It must be done right for everyone's continued safety

Fitness is important. Your officers cannot afford to be out-thought or physically overpowered by a criminal opponent. Encourage them to stay physically and mentally and emotionally fit. Set a great example for them in the manner in which you take care of yourself. Have the courage to say something if you notice one of your folks starting to slide in the manner in which he takes care of himself. You may in the process be saving his or her life.

Remain alert for and respond to the danger signs. Every experienced law enforcement officer has his own list of danger signs based upon his training and (especially) his experience. Spotting them does not automatically translate into the need to respond with force of some degree, although it might, depending upon what was spotted. But detecting one or more danger signs does mean that it is time to increase awareness and change tactics, such as going to cover and summoning assistance. A list of potential hazard warning flags shared by many officers includes the following:

- Hands not visible
- Subject under the influence of drugs or alcohol
- Subject angry or agitated
- Subject disregarding instructions
- Individual hiding or fleeing
- Additional subjects appearing
- Subject trying to move in closer
- Subject verbalizing threats against the officer or himself
- Suspect clinching his fists or taking a "fighting" stance
- Potential weapons visible, such as a knife in a scabbard
- A targeting stare, such as on the officer's holstered handgun
- Movement towards a route of escape

Watch their hands. Emphasize to your officers the importance of keeping the hands of those they are in contact with under close observation. A hidden hand may not be holding a weapon, but it could be. Spotting this potential danger sign obviously does not mean that your cop should start blasting away. But it does mean he should increase his level of awareness and be prepared to implement other officer safety tactics.

Spend time thinking about hypothetical threats and hypothetical responses. No matter how busy they are, your officers have down time on the job, particularly if they are working the overnight shift. Encourage them to use these quiet times to think over hypothetical threats and how they would respond to them. (Example: My partner has been disarmed and the offender is demanding that I surrender my own weapon.) Let your people know that experience has proven that officers who have played threat scenarios through their mind often have responded more effectively when something similar happened for real.

Critique your own safety practices. Your people are watching you, and that's good. You will set an excellent example of officer safety for them. To be sure that you do that you must step back and examine your own safety practices from time to time. Are you getting just a tad sloppy somewhere? Is there a safety skill you need to brush up on? How is your level of physical and emotional fitness? Answering these questions honestly will help assure that you always set a great example of safety and survival for your closely observing subordinates. Doing so also will help you stay safe.

All of these tactics and techniques, if applied by your officers, will make them safer on the job. You will help assure that by observing their safety practices and correcting them where they fall short. But there is more that you can do to help them. You can display a safety-first attitude towards your job and require that your people do the same. You do not tolerate or excuse unsafe behavior. Nor do you accept flimsy excuses for failing to attend officer safety training.

You also will stay in close touch with your employees to determine what is concerning them about their safety on the job. If they have legitimate equipment, policy, or other safety-related worries it will be your job to take them forward to the management level where they can be addressed. At the same time, you will keep a lookout for safety enhancers that may help protect your officers. The safety of your employees and how it might be improved should always be foremost in your mind as you review periodicals, research, and Internet content on officer safety products, tactics, and training.

Making your people safer is a never-ending task for you, their leader. It is one that you are well-equipped to handle.

THE VALUE OF ROLE MODELING

As in virtually everything else you do as a leader, you must serve as an exceptional role model for demonstrated officer safety. Nothing less is acceptable for a law enforcement leader. The attitude and demeanor you exhibit on the job must demonstrate the importance you place on safe practices. Your likewise must display excellent safety and risk management practices in the tasks you carry out in all aspects of your job. You must show careful officer safety practices in the calls and contacts you make or assist your people with on the street. You also must demonstrate good risk management practices in the way you operate a vehicle or make a decision that has the potential of impacting your employer's legal liability—and your own. Your people must always see risk management behavior that you want them to emulate.

The safety-first attitude of an exceptional role model includes readily admitting it when you make a safety-related mistake. In addition to acknowledging the error you will let your people know that you recognize what you should have done instead. If it is possible to fix the mistake, you are obligated to do it.

You additionally role model the officer survival conduct you expect of your employees when you assure that you further your own officer safety training at every opportunity. There is a clear message in this that you are wanting to send: You can never know enough about officer safety and survival. You understand that and expect your subordinates to know it, too.

You consistently serve as a great role model for your officers. You do it in the moral and ethical manner in which you conduct yourself on and off the job. You do it in the customer-friendly manner you model in your interactions with your community's citizens. And you absolutely must do it in your attitudes and practices related to officer safety and risk management. It is perhaps your most valuable tool for assisting your people to stay safe.

ADVOCATING FOR SAFETY

There is still more that you can do as a conscientious leader to help keep your people safe. You can and must represent your officers' safety interests to those inside and outside of the law enforcement organization. That means that you speak up for your officers when they have properly utilized officer safety and survival tactics yet drew unwarranted criticism. If someone is questioning why your cop handcuffed a 16-year-old shoplifter, it is up to you to explain that teens have killed cops, too. If someone is upset because your people cuffed and searched great grandpa who just ten minutes before was threatening to kill everyone in sight, you might want to tell them the story of the 82-year-old traffic offender who murdered two officers with shots to the back of the head. You must be just as forthright and courageous in answering such queries from inside the agency as you are with citizens on the outside. You must be just as up-front with the Chief as you are with Joe the barber.

You must serve as a strong voice for your cops when it comes to safety equipment that should be purchased or policies and procedures that should be implemented or revised for greater officer safety. Volunteer to participate or take the lead in evaluating proposed equipment or writing policies and procedures. You must be willing to show that you are just as willing to take on more work as you are to voice your safety opinions.

Additionally, you need to be willing and capable of serving as a well-informed "educator" on safety matters both within and without your department. Naturally you must be a knowledgeable officer safety trainer for your team of employees. Beyond that you have to be willing tactfully to teach others above you and outside the agency about the very real dangers of the police job and how to mitigate them. That means you cannot be bashful or hesitant to speak up for safety, whether it is in a departmental staff meeting or the Optimist Club downtown.

As a law enforcement officer and leader you are held in high esteem by most solid citizens and community leaders. They are always interested in hearing what you have to say. Use the opportunity, whether it is in a one-on-one conversation or in front of a whole group, to talk about your job and its hazards. As you know, many people are fascinated about police work. Do not overstate your case or exaggerate the very real danger. The truth is scary enough for the average citizen who knows little of your profession beyond what he is told by the mass media. Let these good people know what your officers go through every shift and just what it takes to do a police officer's job today. Do not omit what citizens can do to help, even if it's no more than provide constant support for their guardians through their words and prayers. If you have something more tangible in mind, mention that, too. ("We sure could use more police cars.") But a word of caution: If you have asked a citizens group for more of anything, let your boss know that you have done it. The Brass hate surprises coming in through the back door.

Speak up for safety at every opportunity. Speak up for your people when you know they have done it the right way. When you have done that you will know that you have met another of your most important obligations as a leader.

SUMMARY

By the very nature of your job you should be an expert on the topics of officer safety and risk management. It is necessary that you are such at a time when the average law enforcement officer's well-being is more at risk than at any other time in memory. Through your expertise and by your actions you can make that officer safer on the job.

You support officer survival by carefully observing your subordinates' attention to and practice of safety and risk management. You make it clear to them that they are at least as much at risk from driving their police car too fast as they are from an assailant's bullets. You are always willing to commend safe behavior and correct unsafe practices. Where necessary, you teach the right way to stay safe or you obtain the assistance of qualified others to teach specialized safety skills. Perhaps most important of all, you role model excellent officer safety in your own actions, on and off the street. If you fall short in applying safe practices and tactics you own up to your mistake and make clear that you know what you should have done instead.

Additionally, you speak for your people in all aspects of safety and risk management. If you recognize that a piece of equipment or an established policy or practice is making your people less safe, you are prompt in bringing it to the attention of those in a position to fix it. You offer to help in carrying out that task.

Finally, you serve as a strong, clear voice for your people, your department, and your profession on the urgent subject of officer safety and survival. You serve as an educator for those outside of policing who have little accurate information about the dangers of the police officer's job and the safety practices that can make that job less risky. In so doing you serve as a valuable and credible supporter of doing it the right way, the safe way.

Chapter 10

YOUR ROLE AS COUNSELOR
AND CONFIDANT

It is unlikely that you signed on to a law enforcement career with the intent of becoming a counselor. But if you are like most law enforcement officers you have spent a career offering counseling advice to countless troubled citizen-customers. It's something that you have learned to do pretty well and most likely you are at least relatively comfortable with doing it. Nevertheless, for many leaders the counseling task becomes much harder when the individual to be counseled is a fellow cop, a subordinate, and perhaps a friend.

That does not have to be the case where you are concerned. The skills you apply in counseling citizen-customers can be utilized when you are working with your own employees, too. In addition, the sincere empathy that you display when aiding your community's citizens also will prove especially helpful in assisting your own subordinates.

One of the skills you will apply in working with your people is simply keeping all of your senses attuned for spotting a problem. If you do detect potential trouble you then will apply some of the time- and experience-proven techniques that have helped you assist a lot of puzzled and troubled people over the years. But first you will *listen*, and listen carefully. Meanwhile you will remain aware that there are sources of assistance you can turn to when you need help with a particularly difficult counseling challenge. You are not alone in your efforts. You also will remain aware that "success" in your counseling work can have more than one meaning. You can (and must) realize that ultimate "success" in solving an employee's personal problem lies with that person, not you. You will do your very best to help. The rest is up to the subject of your counseling endeavors.

The whole process begins with realizing that something isn't quite right.

SPOTTING A PROBLEM

In the best of all possible worlds the people-helping process commences when an employee comes to you, his or her boss, and asks for help in solving a vexing, personal issue. It can happen that way, and sometimes it does. That's good. But more often it will take considerably more effort to discover that something is wrong and then determine just what it is and what to do about it. That is where your counselor's skills may get their first real test.

No matter how close you are with your employees there is a very good chance that you will not be the first to notice that something is amiss with one of your people. The fact is that your employees spend more time in the company of and conversing with their co-workers than you do. That is not by any means a condemnation of your leadership style—it's simply a realistic picture of how the work world works. You cannot be everywhere at once and see and hear everything that transpires. As a consequence, you also must depend on your team members to detect a potential problem abuilding and let you know about it.

This will not happen, however, unless you maintain a two-way communication exchange with your subordinates. Unless they trust you enough to talk with you openly, this early warning system will not work. It is going to be tough enough for one of your people to tell you about a problem with one of his or her peers. He or she does not want to anger that peer and be labeled a stoolie. The communication will not occur at all unless your employee really trusts you. If he does approach you, set everything aside and really listen to what he has to say. Be willing to protect his confidentiality if he requests it and you agree that it is appropriate. Thank your employee for trusting you enough to share his observations and concerns. It likely required both courage on his part and trust in you for him to share the information. Let him know that you will continue to be accessible.

An employee who has brought you a concern about a colleague must be assured by you that you will act on his observation, even if your initial action involves only heightened awareness and close attention. You do not want to minimize his concerns but neither do you wish to overreact. If you do either you may find that you do not have an employee willing to come forward again. It is also important to remember that the actual situation may not be what was suspected and reported. The rumor mill could have contributed to or exaggerated the actual scenario. Honest, good faith mistakes sometimes are made by concerned peers, as well. Be sure you have the facts as well as it is possible to know them before you approach the concerned employee or plan a course of action. It's possible you won't have sufficient information until you have done some observing of your own and talked with the employee who is at the center of the concerns. Experience has taught you that things are not always as they initially appear.

Equally important are your own observations of employee behavior. But exactly what are you looking for to help identify a subordinate who may need assistance? There are, of course, some obvious signs that something is bothering Joe (Example: he experiences an emotional meltdown for no apparent reason right in the middle of the roll call briefing). Obviously, Joe has an issue and could use your empathy and offer of help. Other less-obvious warning indicators that further investigation is required may include the following:

Major change in at-work demeanor. The employee who is always outgoing and jovial who suddenly becomes (and stays) moody or short-tempered may be signaling the presence of a serious problem of one kind or another. The same holds true for the officer who is talkative and upbeat who gradually or overnight becomes a silent introvert. Further inquiry would be well-advised.

Complaints from fellow employees or citizens. Most people, cops and citizen-customers included, are often willing to overlook a certain amount of rude or brusque behavior, if for no other reason than the effort required to report it. When one or more of your employees or citizens of the community complain on more than one occasion about bad behavior by one of your people you are obliged to investigate. The more complaints that are received the greater your concern should be. It's likely that something is going on.

Evidence of drug or alcohol abuse. It almost goes without saying: the police employee who shows up for work under the influence of alcohol or drugs—prescription or otherwise—must be removed from duty and transported safely home or for medical care, whichever is indicated. Prompt follow-up is required of you, his or her supervisor.

This danger flag also may indicate a violation of the law and (almost certainly) the agency's rules and regulations. It's serious business.

Increased absences or instances of tardiness. When the employee who has been punctual in the past and hardly ever missed a day of work starts coming in late or not showing up at all something other than illness may be at the root of the problem. Once you have eliminated actual illness as the cause further investigation is a must. Certainly, inquiry must be made and help should be proffered, but the conduct cannot be allowed to continue. The rest of the team deserves better.

Deteriorating quality and/or quantity of work. The star or even average performer who displays a drastic downturn in work performance likely is signaling that something is not right. Just what that something might be is up to his supervisor—you—to find out. There has got to be an explanation and there just may be a significant problem involved. But you probably won't know for sure until you do some digging.

Frequent emotional outbursts. Repeated, uncharacteristic, uncontrolled bursts of emotion, particularly anger, are practically guaranteed to herald some sort of personal problem or condition afflicting your employee. Inquiry and action are mandatory for you. As you know, ignoring the symptoms of a problem could allow something worse to happen with an employee who has access to firearms.

Increased instances of use of force. Repeated, frequent uses of force by an officer may be simply coincidence. But they may not be, particularly in the case of the cop who has seldom had to use force previously. Immediate inquiry is indicated. The instances could be tied to a shortening of temper or other emotional turmoil in your officer. For both his good and that of the community he may need temporarily removed from contact with the public. Dealing effectively with this situation must be a priority for you and your agency.

Insubordinate behavior. Employees who are part of a law enforcement organization know how they are expected to interact with their supervisors. An employee who has strayed into insubordinate behavior, particularly on repeated occasions, is showing he cannot control his impulses or doesn't care enough to do so. Either way he is telegraphing the presence of a serious problem. For the good of the employee and the organization immediate investigation and action are needed.

Deteriorating hygiene, dress, and grooming. The trooper who has always appeared neat and squared away who suddenly gives the appearance that he just doesn't care is almost certainly going through difficulties of some kind. He or she may even be seeking your attention. Don't disappoint.

The employee avoids contact with you. Many employees had rather do their jobs than hob nob with their boss. There's nothing wrong with that. But when it appears that one of your people is deliberately going to a lot of effort to stay away from you there may be a reason that you need to know about. The behavior clearly bears investigating. If he is simply angry with you for some reason you need to clear the air about that, too.

Family members or friends express concerns to you. As any supervisor who has gotten a call from an employee's spouse or loved one can attest, the news is often not good and it's time to pay close attention to what the caller has to say. Something is bothering that loved one enough to risk their partner's wrath by contacting his or her boss. Try to be sensitive and empathetic towards the caller as you carefully listen to his or her concern. It's alright to probe gently for further information.

Of course, there are additional signs and symptoms that a personal problem is troubling one of your employees. Some of these listed indicators, taken alone and not repeated, do not necessarily indicate the presence of a serious problem. For example, the employee who shows up for work hung over from the night before may be exhibiting the effects of some unwise over-partying that has not occurred previously and will not be repeated. You do not want to overreact to a single, apparently isolated incident. But you DO want to increase the attention you pay to that subordinate until you know more about what may be going on. Intervention may or may not be required.

The more behavioral warning signs you observe the stronger the evidence that you have an employee with a problem that demands your attention. The frequency with which these red flags are spotted and the intensity of the behavior are also important to note. Waiting too long to intervene may permit a problem to worsen, perhaps with increasingly hazardous consequences.

Having now decided that intervention is necessary, what do you do next? Just how do you go about doing it? Some intervention tactics and techniques that have worked well for other supervisor-counselors may work equally well for you. . . .

SOME PROBLEM-SOLVING TECHNIQUES

As any professional counselor would tell you, there are a handful of basic rules for working with a counselee. Concisely put, they include the following:

1. Shut up and listen
2. Do not interrupt
3. Don't express surprise, shock, or disgust
4. Refrain from jumping instantly into problem-solving mode
5. Don't be judgmental
6. Listen some more

Each of these basic rules should apply to your own counselling efforts focused on your law enforcement employees. They are basic and require little or no further explanation. There are additional counselling guidelines that may prove helpful, as well. While every counseling opportunity will be at least somewhat different from the last, here are some tips that have worked well for other law enforcement leaders-turned-counselors:

Be sure you have your facts straight at the outset. It is unlikely that you will know everything there is to know about what is troubling your employee before you sit down with him or her. But gather as much information as you can ahead of your meeting. You will lose credibility and aggravate your employee if you confront him with information that is factually incorrect. For that reason alone, you do not want to act on rumors and uncorroborated tales. Whenever possible base your meeting on your own observations and fact-gathering. It is also alright to admit to your employee that you do not have the full story on what is going on but you are concerned and need his help in figuring out what is happening.

Find a private space and time. You will need a private place where you will not be interrupted while meeting with your employee. If possible, it should be well away from other employees who will detect the closed-door meeting and start to spread tales that "something is going on." Neither you nor your employee should be pressed for time. The session should take just as much time as required, whatever that may be. There should be no yapping portable radios or ringing cell phones permitted.

Be up front about the purpose of the meeting. A few pleasantries are fine, but your employee likely knows the purpose of the meeting. It accomplishes little to put off getting to the purpose of the sit-down, so get to it. Lead off by letting him know that you are concerned about his welfare and want to help if you can. Do not be surprised if you get an initial denial that anything is amiss. You can repeat your concerns, if need be, but don't beat around the bush.

Take your time. It is worth saying again. It is understandable that the session may be uncomfortable for the both of you and you both are anxious to get it over with. But slow down and stick with it. Let your employee know that you have all the time in the world for the meeting. False deadlines should not be a cause for abandoning your efforts at helping. Your employee should not be allowed to think that you will back off due to time constraints.

Seek good eye contact and avoid distractions. This is not a staring contest, but neither should you look at your shoes or the wall throughout most of the meeting. Make good eye contact and face your employee. Your posture should be relaxed to the extent possible. Avoid nervous habits such as fiddling with a pen or pencil. Focus on your employee instead. Be alert for distractions that the employee may attempt to create to get away from an uncomfortable topic ("How 'bout them crazy politicians?") Gently steer your subordinate back to the issue at hand.

Focus on behavior, not the individual. Your counseling conversation with your employee should include a lot of "I's" ("I am concerned; I am worried") and few references to "you." "You" tends to bring with it blame for something. It should be made clear to your associate that you believe he is a good person and a good employee, but something in his current performance is troubling you.

Keep the conversation focused. You need to allow your employee to talk freely. But there is a balance to be maintained. At the same time, if he heads off down a path that clearly has nothing to do with the current situation you need to steer him back to the purpose of the meeting. It's ok to tell him that's what you are doing. The two of you can talk about that seemingly unrelated event another time.

Be sure the employee has the freedom to talk. Let your subordinate know that he is free to talk openly, even if what he has to say is critical of you, the department, or the Big Boss. You can and should let him know that your conversation will not be broadcast to his peers but you should not promise total confidentiality before you know what he is going to tell you. If he tells you that he is thinking about killing his spouse you obviously cannot keep that a secret.

Make it clear that you want to help. That should be your opening to your subordinate. You should not focus on productivity statistics or anything similar. You should emphasize that you want to help solve an apparent problem, not get more productivity out of him or her. The fact that you want to help should begin and conclude your counseling session.

Be prepared for an emotional response. One veteran police supervisor makes certain that he has a box of tissues in the room before he begins a counseling session, regardless of the gender or age of his employee. Your employee may react strongly to what you have to say, with emotions ranging from anger to embarrassment. Be sensitive to his or her feelings, but do not allow the display of emotion to divert you from your task. Remember, too, that most cops are good actors. The emotions you are confronting are most likely genuine, but they also could be intended to get you to back away. Take a break if emotions are distracting from the session, but resume after a short interruption. Meanwhile, keep your own emotions in check. You should not, for example, meet anger with anger of your own. Avoid an overdose of authority, too. Your employee already knows that you are the boss. Even if your employee's actions have aggravated you in the extreme, remember that this is not a disciplinary meeting. Save your "I'm really angry" face for another occasion.

Know that you may have to try again. In spite of your best efforts your employee may deny, perhaps emotionally, that anything is amiss or needs changing. Do not insist that the employee must accept that something is wrong. Repeat that you are concerned, then be prepared to return to the topic again. The prime time to do this will be when and if the aberrant behavior occurs again. Be persistent. On occasion, the problem will be resolved and will not recur even though the employee denies that it ever existed. Your initial effort was sufficient to spur the needed change in behavior. Mission achieved.

Let your counselee know that you are always available. Be sure your employee knows that this is not the only time the two of you can talk. Assure him that he can contact you any time, on-duty or off, should the need arise. Your intention is to let your team member know that you really *do* care and are willing to go the extra mile to help, whatever that requires. Then, check with him later to see how things are going. Keep monitoring his actions, as well. There may be a need for the two of you to talk again. As you know, many problems are not resolved after the first attempt at a solution.

Offer some other options whenever possible. Your employee may be embarrassed to open up to you or he may feel that you do not have the expertise to help him. You may agree with that assessment. For that reason, you should be prepared to offer him some alternatives for follow-up help. It could be Alcoholics Anonymous or a mental health counseling service or one of a dozen other resources depending upon the problem or problems involved. It will be worthwhile for you to keep a list of potential professional helpers in your area. Share it with your troubled employee. Follow-up with him to see if he has made the connection.

Summarize the issue and seek agreement on a solution. Whenever feasible the counseling session should conclude with you summarizing the issue being confronted and what the two of you have agreed to do about it. If there is no agreement that a problem exists, that should be noted, too. Emphasize that you are always available to talk again. Your employee just might change his mind about letting you in on his difficulties. Let him know that you remain concerned about the presence of a possible problem.

Reinforce the fact that you care. After an intense and possibly emotional meeting it is just possible that your employee may have lost sight of the purpose of the sit-down. Remind him again that you care and want to see everything work out well for him. Remind him that you are always available to talk. Let him know if you are planning a follow-up meeting. If he has done something positive lately, do not hesitate to mention it and thank him for it as a "oh, by the way" comment. Where possible it's always good to end on a positive note.

Assuming that the employee is willing to talk freely with you, realize that he or she may not expect you to solve the problem or otherwise act. Your employee may just want you to listen and express empathy. This you are certainly capable of doing. While you do want to help, be sure that you do not promise a solution that you cannot or should not deliver. An example may be found in the employee who states the belief that all will be right in his world if he can just get moved off of the midnight shift. Unless you have the ultimate authority to grant his wish and know that you will not cause harm for the organization or someone else by doing so, do not pledge to move him to the day shift. He is not going to be pleased when he discovers you cannot deliver on your promise. Your credibility will have just taken a big hit.

Remember, too, that none of the tactics and techniques previously described can be guaranteed to work in every instance. Each situation and individual are different from every other. You know that. You also may need to let go of a situation temporarily when the subject employee refuses to talk with you and/or adamantly denies that a problem exists. But you will not hesitate to broach the issue again. The good news is that you do not have to shoulder the load by yourself.

YOU DON'T HAVE TO GO IT ALONE

There are resources out there that can help you handle a counseling challenge. You are going to encounter situations that you are not trained to approach unassisted. You are not the right one to assist an employee with a drug or alcohol dependency problem, for instance. Neither are you a marriage counselor or a financial affairs expert. But there are talented people who specialize in handling all of these things. It may be that you can best aid your team member by pointing him in the right direction to obtain professional help. You can then help further by following up and being a nag, if need be, to see that he is actually working with an appropriate professional.

There is even more help available to you, and it is close at hand. You likely can obtain advice and assistance from your colleagues if you just ask for their help. One or more of them may have dealt with a situation very similar to the one you are facing now. Your own boss also may have an idea or suggestion. It is a good idea to let your supervisor know anyway that you are dealing with a personnel issue, although it is not necessary to go into great detail except in the most exceptional cases. Again: bosses don't like surprises.

You already realize that there may not be a perfect solution to an employee's difficulties. But your agency's resources may be able to provide you with advice on what to do next. Avail yourself of the expertise offered by peer support programs, police psychologists, and employee assistance programs if any of them are available through your employer. Even better, steer your troubled employee to these sources of professional help. Let him know that no stigma will be attached to asking for professional help when it is needed. You might note that he would seek professional help if his leg was broken. This is no different. The key for him is being smart enough to accept that he needs help and courageous enough to seek it. With patience and persistence you may be able to help him reach that realization.

You are never alone when it comes to seeking help for a troubled law enforcement employee. There is help available. You need only seek to identify it. It is the obligation of the employee to make the connection for appropriate assistance when more expertise than his supervisor can provide is needed. With sincere effort on the part of your employee the situation WILL improve.

WHAT IS SUCCESS?

"Success" is something different for every instance and individual. There may be varying degrees of it. A problem may be reduced in intensity but not completely solved. This is a good time to state the by-now obvious once again: You as a leader cannot solve everything for everyone. You can and should try to help as much as possible. But the problem solution remains with the individual experiencing the difficulty, whatever it may be.

It will be helpful for both you and your counselee to identify the result you are seeking. For the perpetually late employee it may be consistently getting where he is supposed to be when he is supposed to be there, regardless of the nature of the factors making him habitually tardy. It is primarily up to him to identify and deal with those factors. For the officer who has trouble controlling his temper, it may be an anger management class plus work on the personal issues that are the driving force behind his bad behavior. Whatever the case, the onus is on the employee, not you, to solve the problem. Neither of you should forget that.

"Success" in some instances may mean that the negatives are mitigated, not eradicated. Sometimes that may be the best to be hoped for. "Success" also may not be achieved at the first try. You and your counselee may need to keep working at it and try again. And again. Progress may be slow in coming. Once more, the primary responsibility for problem mitigation remains with the employee, not his or her supervisor.

As in your employee performance review responsibilities, follow-up will be required once an employee problem has been identified and addressed. Are you seeing continued improvement, or has any bettering of the situation been temporary in nature? Is more work needed? By staying in contact with your employee—ask him how he thinks he is doing—you can determine if success is passing or lasting. Do not be hesitant to speak up if you are not seeing the needed change maintained. That's required of a leader, too. Neither should you neglect to award deserved praise for real and maintained progress. The simple act of recognizing good work can make both of you feel good.

SUMMARY

You are an empathetic and caring professional. You have demonstrated those traits throughout your law enforcement career. It is not surprising, then, that you display them in spades when the individual needing help is one of your own employees.

You do your job well as a counselor-confidant when you maintain a constant surveillance for problems arising among the members of your crew. Some of this you accomplish through personal observation, much of the rest you do by maintaining open communication with the members of your team who may spot a problem before you do. You then exercise the confidence and courage required to approach the employee exhibiting symptoms of a problem and engage him or her in a nonthreatening but honest conversation. You are open, you are empathetic, but you are wise enough never to promise confidentiality until and unless you know the full nature and ramifications of the personal difficulty. You desire to help but you will not be party to any sort of unethical coverup.

You will apply your best counseling skills and look for additional assistance when your common sense and knowledge of the situation tell you that you need it. You will monitor your employee and follow-up with him, as required. You will, in other words, continue to care. All the same you will never forget that you cannot solve anyone else's issues for him or her. You will do everything you reasonably can to help. Ultimately, however, the responsibility for problem-solving success remains with the employee himself. You must not forget that.

You are a kind and caring leader. You have established that over a career of helping diverse others. It is highly likely that you will do a pretty good job of serving as a counselor-confidant for your team members, too.

Chapter 11

YOUR OBLIGATION AS DISCIPLINARIAN

For very many employees and for too many supervisors the term "discipline" is associated primarily with punishment. It should thus come as no surprise that for subordinates and supervisors alike the whole disciplinary process too often reeks of negativism and is to be avoided if at all possible.

The reality is that discipline involves much more than correction for something done wrong. After all, discipline in its most noble form refers to *self-discipline,* the internally-generated drive to do the right thing for the right reason. The self-disciplined individual does not toe the line because he or she fears painful consequences. An exceptional leader displays self-discipline in his or her job performance and personal life. It is there for subordinates and anyone else to see, admire, and, hopefully, emulate.

Still, discipline refers to more than admirable behavior. It also can include training, coaching, and counseling to help a law enforcement employee overcome personal weaknesses and become a more effective practitioner of his or her chosen profession. This is sometimes referred to as *positive discipline.*

But the realities of the world dictate that at times positive forms of discipline are inadequate or otherwise inappropriate, as in the case of a repeated or major transgression, and more punitive discipline must be applied. For that kind of discipline to be appropriate and achieve its desired goal of changed behavior the first-line supervisor must be intimately involved. This chapter is devoted to helping you serve ethically, compassionately, and effectively in the role of disciplinarian when any kind of discipline, but especially negative or corrective discipline, is required.

WHY DISCIPLINE AT ALL?

So, if discipline is such a difficult and often-unpleasant experience for everyone involved, why do it in the first place? To put it succinctly, because it is part of your job if you aspire to be an effective and ethical leader. It is what leaders do in addition to the myriad other tasks that they ably perform.

As a law enforcement officer, you believe strongly in justice. It's why you do what you do every day or night. You have accepted working in the furtherance of justice as your duty. You also have a duty—an obligation, if you will—to your employees, your colleagues, your boss, your organization, and the community to assure that your subordinates are doing the job they are paid to do as effectively and efficiently as possible. Sometimes that means you must take corrective action to bring their job performance to an acceptable level. As you know, effective law enforcement requires a team effort. If one or more of your people is causing disruptions to the work or otherwise not shouldering their fair share of the load, the rest of the team as well as the citizens you all serve are being shortchanged. That is something that you as a leader are obliged to prevent from occurring or fix when it does occur. Sometimes "fixing" requires disciplinary intervention of one kind or another.

Depending on the nature of the misconduct or other shortfall in job performance, you may be able successfully to address the issue through counseling or additional training. Sometimes that is referred to as *positive discipline*. But on occasion positive discipline does not have the desired corrective effect. Or the transgression or other performance issue is so serious that more drastic measures—such as a letter of reprimand or leave without pay—must be taken. That is sometimes referenced as *negative discipline*. It is also possible that both positive and negative discipline will be applied in response to the same performance issue. In this case the employee may be counseled (by you), assigned to attend additional training, and suspended without pay for a set period of time. An example may be found in the case of the officer who has just experienced his third at-fault vehicle accident this year.

There is yet another very human reason that you must discipline when lack of appropriate job performance or other employee misconduct is proven to have occurred: If you fail to deal with the bad, you risk losing the good. Doubtlessly you have heard some version of this very legitimate warning before. Your people know which of your team members are doing their jobs and which ones are not. If the workers conclude that you are not confronting the non-workers they may lose faith in you as their leader. Their logic may go something like this: I am doing my job, busting my hump and risking my life every day while Lazy Larry dodges assignments and otherwise does as little as possible. If I keep doing what I am doing with no relief in sight I am some kind of chump. So, in the future I am going to do it Larry's way. When that happens you have just lost a productive member of your team. Other members may shortly follow suit unless you intervene and deal with Lazy Larry. If you fail to act you may lose your team, one member at a time. Eventually that is going to be noticed well beyond the team. Then you are going to have some tough explaining to do to your own boss. That's not a scenario you want to have happen. By doing your job as leader and, when necessary, disciplinarian, you will never have to face that unpleasant session.

Correcting employee performance issues is one of your most important responsibilities as a leader. It is part of your job. The next topic for discussion is how to do it well.

DOING IT THE RIGHT WAY

"The right way" can mean a lot of things. When it comes to discipline, correctness calls for touching several bases on the way to a successful outcome. That outcome likely will call for corrected or improved job performance by the subject of the discipline.

There is another benefit of discipline done right. Discipline is at least as much for the rest of the organization as it is for the direct recipient. It sets out for everyone what is and is not acceptable conduct. It lets all hands know the potential consequences of doing it "the wrong way." That in itself is a powerful and valuable lesson that can make the whole organization better. When you discipline, you are helping to send that message.

There are a number of steps involved in selecting and administering discipline that is appropriate, balanced, and just. Those guidelines include the following:

Get the full story before you act. Having to undo a disciplinary action because you did not have your facts straight is not something any supervisor wants to go through. Be certain you have all the relevant facts in hand before you decide on and implement a course of action. You also will want to be aware of any mitigating factors. Any explanations the employee may offer for the event should be heard, as well. If something tells you that things are not right, delay the discipline until you are certain of your facts.

Don't put it off unnecessarily. You want to get it right, but that is not a valid excuse to put off doing what may feel like an unpleasant task. Procrastinating will not make the job any easier. Getting it over with may make both you and the discipline's recipient feel better at having the thing done. Take as much time as you need in the disciplinary meeting itself; just don't wait too long to initiate the session.

If necessary, get advice from your colleagues. Puzzled at what you should do with the information you have and the action you should take? It's absolutely acceptable (and advisable) to seek the experience and advice of your peers who may have dealt with a similar disciplinary situation. You are not bound to do what anyone else has done, but talking with your colleagues may give you an idea if you are in the right ballpark with the discipline you have in mind. Your agency's disciplinary records also may be helpful in providing insight into what has been done in the past.

Find out what has gone on before with the employee. Your agency's records should tell you about the subject employee's past actions, good and bad. They should tell you if this is his "first offense" or if he has been guilty of improper conduct previously. You are likely going to be more lenient with an excellent employee who has stumbled for the first time as opposed to a chronic offender. The employee's previous supervisor also may be able to fill you in on his or her previous performance.

Determine if it is a mistake of head or heart. A mistake of the head occurs when, say, an officer oversleeps and misses a court appearance for the first time. A mistake of the heart happens when an officer who wants to play golf rather than go to court intentionally misses the trial or hearing—for the fourth time. The latter officer should, barring any "special" circumstances, receive a more serious disciplinary response. A mistake of the heart often involves intent or serious negligence, while a mistake of the head frequently comes from not knowing any better or making an honest mistake. Lying to a supervisor would constitute a very serious mistake of the heart. The disciplinary response might well be terminal in nature.

Be sure you have the necessary approvals for formal disciplinary action. It will be more than a little embarrassing if you have to take back a disciplinary action because your boss did not approve of it. To keep that from happening be sure that you have his or her blessing before you take a significant disciplinary action, such as a suspension without pay. Your boss may have an insight on the whole matter that you have missed. Your approach should be that you are letting your supervisor know in advance what you plan to do, not that you are seeking his permission. He will let you know if he thinks you are off-base. He also just may want more information. Be prepared to supply it.

Be sure discipline is consistent and otherwise defensible. The discipline you have in mind should approximate what has been done before in similar situations. This is sometimes referred to as *comparative discipline,* and it is intended to ensure that for similar improper behavior Bobby draws the same penalty as Susie, and the other way around, assuming that their past performance also has been similar and there are no extenuating circumstances. The objective is that you and your agency can successfully defend the discipline if it is challenged in a civil court or disciplinary appeal hearing.

Remember that discipline must be progressive. In other words, you should not dispatch the proverbial fly with the proverbial hammer for a "first offense." But repeated misconduct, particularly if it is of a serious nature, should draw a harsher penalty each time it occurs. In other words, the corrective action should become progressively stronger. In some agencies, minor infractions may first draw a counseling session and warning. The second infraction may result in a letter of reprimand, and the third a suspension without pay. But there are exceptions, of course. Maybe Joe received a warning after he accidentally nicked the side of his patrol car for the first time. Iggy would be foolish to expect similar discipline for *his* first accident that just happened to involve his totaling two cars and injuring two citizens as the at-fault driver. *Consequences* of inappropriate conduct are always part of the equation.

Assure that a disciplinary meeting is done in private. The old maxim about praising in public and correcting in private is applicable here. An employee's disciplinary meeting with you is a personal matter and the disciplinary meeting needs to be held in private. While he may decide to broadcast his version of the meeting to his peers it is not your role to do so. Your boss needs to know the outcome of the meeting if he asks; the world at large does not.

Anticipate an emotional response and keep your own emotions in check. Your past experience with him or her may provide a hint as to how that individual is likely to react in a disciplinary meeting. You might or might not be right about what to expect, but realize that emotions often run high anytime discipline is to be assessed. Keep your own composure even in the face of loud and emotional opposition. Try to be empathetic as well as tactful and patient. It is not necessary to scream that you are the boss and what you say goes. The employee already knows that. Allow the employee to vent within reason, if that's what he elects to do. But do not back down from what you know to be the correct course of action.

Do not apologize for doing your job. Expressing empathy is fine, but that's where it stops. You should never express regret or remorse for doing your job as a disciplinarian. Your employee knows, or should know, that discipline is one of your responsibilities. You also should not make light of what was, in fact, a significant violation of your agency's expectations. It's alright to let your employee know that you realize this incident was not characteristic of him (if that's true), but that's as far as it should go. The burden properly should be on him, not you, for any apologies.

Own your actions. Never blame a disciplinary action on someone else. That is a cardinal rule for an appropriately courageous leader. Let your employee know that you are the source of the discipline and that you feel it is just for the particulars of the case. Only cowards try to lay the "blame" elsewhere. You are no coward.

Be clear as to your expectations. Your employee needs to have a clear picture of what you expect of him for the future. Draw it for him. It is also alright to let him know up front what will happen next if the improper action is repeated. Let him know that you will monitor his performance and acknowledge any progress he makes. Then, follow through with your pledge to praise him when praise is earned.

Document what happened. Make a written record of what you did and why following any disciplinary action. A problem sometimes can be found in an organization's disciplinary process when multiple supervisors "forgive" a first mistake by an employee and make no record of it. As the employee moves through different supervisors and commits several more "first" violations and more supervisors give him a pass for that first one he has built up quite a record—except that he doesn't have one. It's fine to forgive, but it is unwise to forget, at least when it comes to documentation. Write it down. Doing so may turn out to be very important if the problems continue or become more serious.

Follow-up to be certain that needed change occurs. Discipline should not be done and promptly forgotten. As a leader you are responsible for monitoring the disciplined employee's performance to assure that the problem has truly been resolved. Further supervisory action may be needed. The employee also needs to be credited for resolving the problem if that is indeed the case. Let hm or her know what you have observed.

Realize that an appeal does not mean you have erred. In some public safety agencies employees are almost automatic in appealing their discipline, regardless of how much they may have deserved it and how appropriate it may be. If you have crafted your disciplinary response appropriately the chances that it will be overturned are reduced considerably. Realize, too, that someone in the review and appeal chain may have a very legitimate reason for modifying the discipline, if for no other reason than to show "mercy." It is perfectly acceptable to ask why your boss (or his boss) altered your discipline. You may learn something useful in the process. But keep in mind that, absent your being told something to the contrary, there is no reason to believe that you made a mistake. This represents one more instance in which you need to be confident in your decision-making.

Learn from every disciplinary process. As in all your other responsibilities as a leader, you learn from your experience in handling disciplinary matters. Your intent should be to gain knowledge from this one to even better handle the next one, which almost inevitably will come. As in so many aspects of your job, you get better at it by doing it. As that experience grows you will find that one day your peers are coming to *you* for disciplinary advice.

Every disciplinary situation is different from the last or the next. An approach that worked well in one instance may not be as effective in another. That's alright; the knowledge you gain from each experience will add to your abilities to handle all oncoming disciplinary challenges. You also have been around long enough to know that there are dysfunctional people out there with whom no imaginable approach will work well. Take the necessary action and move on. You must spend most of your time and effort on the employees who will be responsive to your good faith efforts, even if they do not totally agree with the disciplinary outcome. That is the right thing and the best thing that you can do.

THE RESULTS YOU ARE SEEKING

To put it concisely, discipline's purpose is to make everyone better. Discipline helps ensure the good health of the entire law enforcement organization. Whenever possible, those good results are obtained via self-discipline. When more negative discipline must be applied, every member of the organization learns vicariously what is and isn't acceptable behavior and the consequences of engaging in inappropriate or substandard conduct. Effective discipline is thereby educational, too.

Whether it is through counseling, training, coaching, or negative discipline, your goal is to work with your employees to achieve efficient, effective law enforcement service delivery. In some instances, you must utilize a form of discipline to secure changed behavior in an employee. Your objective is to achieve a long-term improvement in job performance, but first you must see it in short-term changes. Your follow-up is intended to assure that the change continues. When that happens, there are multiple beneficiaries. The taxpayers get the results they are paying for. Your organization functions more smoothly. The other members of your work group know that each of their peers is shouldering his or her part of the load and not engaging in conduct that embarrasses the rest of the team. And the employee at the heart of the issue hopefully has the satisfaction of knowing that he or she is a fully contributing member of the team and is valued at such.

Discipline works best when both its recipient and the other members of the work group and the organization regard it as fair and appropriate to the situation. In the best of all possible worlds the subject of the discipline accepts it as fair, balanced, and just, also. A problem has been solved and everyone involved benefits. That is the "best of all possible worlds" scenario. It can indeed play out exactly that way. You recognize that it cannot always work out in that fashion. But when it does everything works better.

Even when it doesn't turn out exactly that way you have done your job well and confronted a personnel problem that had to be solved. If someone in the "audience," most especially the recipient employee, does not accept the discipline as appropriate that is unfortunate but acceptable. A problem is still solved, assuming the expected change in performance occurs. If it does not, further supervisory action, most likely discipline, will need to be applied. That task will fall to you as the leader involved. You can do it just as you have handled the disciplinary process up to this point.

Discipline can be a complex process. It can be difficult, as well. Doubtlessly you never thought it would be easy. But by doing your part you can assure that your people and your organization function at maximum effectiveness and efficiency. That's a pretty big accomplishment for a leader, which is what you clearly are.

SUMMARY

As should be evident by now, discipline it its multiple forms is an important element of the law enforcement supervisor's work life. Discipline in the form of the supervisor's own self-discipline is displayed both on and off the job. That's as it should be for an exemplary leader.

As a leader you have a responsibility to discipline. That obligation affects your subordinates, your organization, the community, and the law enforcement profession. The goal is to make the employee better in his or her role as a service-providing peacekeeper. This chapter provided guidance on how to do discipline well. It covered things to be avoided as well as done in order to ensure discipline that is appropriate, fair, and effective, whether it involves counseling or a week off without pay. Changed behavior and/or performance is the ultimate aim of discipline. Ideally the change should be long-term in nature.

Your disciplinary actions require both competence and courage. Your goal is always that the recipient of the discipline accepts it as just and fair. But you are savvy enough to realize that this will not always be the case. Regardless, you have a job to do and you will do it to the best of your ability. That's a basic requirement for an ethical and effective law enforcement leader.

The talented police supervisor recognizes the benefit to both employee and organization of appropriate discipline, whether that discipline results in counseling, training, or a sanction that costs the individual time, money, or both. That leader likewise realizes the importance of being involved personally in the decision-making contained in every disciplinary process. He knows the difference between an honest mistake of the head and a more troubling mistake of the heart. He awards discipline accordingly. He then follows up to assure that the desired change in performance takes place and continues into the future.

You are that "talented police supervisor." You can do this and do it well. You accept the task as your obligation to be a fair and competent disciplinarian. Discipline is that important to everyone involved.

Chapter 12

THE "DIFFICULT" EMPLOYEE

You know who they are. He sits in the same chair in the back of the briefing room during every roll call. His yakking and complaining regularly interrupt the meeting. That is, when he is not sulking, pouting, and making everyone around him uneasy. He is every sergeant's pain in the neck.

She never ceases telling anyone who will listen how miserable she is and how she has been ill-treated by most everyone in the department from the chief on down. As she tells it, her career and her happiness have been stymied by an unfeeling, uncaring agency. She hints that her revenge is coming soon.

These individuals, whose type can be found in most every organization, law enforcement included, can be a major supervisory challenge. For some supervisors, they amount to a true nightmare. As disruptive as they might be, they may be on the plain vanilla end of the "problem employee" spectrum. Their more extremist, difficult cousins may have escalated their problematic behavior into abusing arrestees, regularly insulting citizens, engaging in plainly insubordinate behavior, flagrantly violating departmental regulations, and even breaking the law. THAT is "difficult" on steroids. All of these problem employees must be effectively handled by a healthy organization with competent and caring leaders.

As you know by now, problem employees cannot be allowed to continue to infect an organization while leaders do little or nothing to intervene. At some point the people who are continuing to do the work the right way will question why they are bothering to do so in an organization where "problem people" are allowed to continue to disrupt and otherwise misbehave. Eventually the whole body of the organization will be sickened by this spreading infection. When that happens leadership effectively has abdicated the responsibility to lead. The organization itself may go into a steady decline that only will be reversed by drastic action. That action not infrequently results in new leadership. If this picture appears a dismal one the truth is that it has happened time after time in the real world. Sometimes law enforcement organizations have been the subject of the disaster.

The good news is that this dark scenario is not destined to occur anywhere, most certainly not within your law enforcement agency. It can be forestalled from developing or cured if already present by courageous leaders who are not hesitant to do the right thing. You must be one of those talented and courageous leaders.

It is unlikely that your own organization is overrun by the sort of problems just described. But yours would be the exceptional organization indeed if absolutely none of these poisonous people is to be found residing there. You as a leader are expected by your organization to deal with each one of your own agency's problem children, where they exist, and address their problematical behavior. It will require the application of all of your skills as a counselor, disciplinarian, and, most of all, a leader. It is unlikely that you will find a "one size fits all" solution in dealing with the problem employee. But by applying the things you already have learned and are learning now about effective leadership you will be able successfully to confront this latest of the numerous challenges you have faced and mastered. You can deal effectively with the "problem" employee.

UNIQUE PEOPLE, UNIQUE CHALLENGES

There are all kinds of "difficult" employees and challenging behaviors inhabiting today's work world. You doubtlessly would concur that a law enforcement employee who is intentionally, flagrantly, and perhaps repeatedly violating his employer's rules, regulations, policies, and procedures definitely could be labelled a "difficult" employee, if not something much worse. The same would hold true for the employee who is actually violating the laws of his jurisdiction and the ethics of his profession. But there are other varieties of problematic behavior that do not necessarily amount to actual, unlawful misconduct that are nonetheless contrary to everything that you as an ethical law enforcement practitioner and leader hold dear. Those behaviors include those on the following but incomplete list:

- Bullying or otherwise maltreating fellow employees
- Belittling and ridiculing arrestees and other accused violators
- Being chronically discourteous and disrespectful to citizen-customers
- Becoming enraged or otherwise aggressively upset for little or no cause
- Being insubordinate towards supervisors
- Yelling, throwing things, and slamming doors when upset
- Threatening to sue or otherwise retaliate when confronted by supervisors
- Consistently and intentionally turning out a substandard work product

This kind of bad behavior can make it unlikely that a colleague of such a toxic individual will want to come to work. It can leave a member of the community with a highly negative opinion of the entire law enforcement organization and less likely to reach out for help again. This sort of behavior is clearly unacceptable in a professional law enforcement agency. Perhaps the only thing worse is for that agency to fail to deal with the misconduct with the goal of eliminating it. As you are aware, left unchecked the bad behavior will not only continue but likely get worse as the "difficult" employee learns that he will be allowed to get away with it. That is a situation that, if left uncorrected long enough, can prove contagious to other employees and ultimately result in the failure of the entire organization. It's *that* serious.

You as a leader will be called upon to stop or otherwise "fix" the unacceptable behavior of the troubling employee. This will remain the expectation even if previous supervisors have failed to resolve the problem. It is in your hands now. One of your early goals will be to find out, if possible, the cause for the disruptive behavior by one of your organization's employees. Why is he or she being "difficult" in the first place? Are there contributing factors? Are there marital issues, alcoholism, mental illness, or other factors in play here? You may not be able to determine the answer, but you still must resolve the problem. None of these potential contributing factors will, of course, excuse problematical behavior. But they may help explain why it is taking place and provide you with some help in determining a solution. Remember all the while, however, that it is the employee, not you, who retains the ultimate responsibility for solving the problem that he or she is causing. He or she needs to know that, too.

You may be able to help answer your questions about possible causative factors by looking for documentation in your agency's personnel and other records. Other supervisors may have had experience with the employee and can inform you about their observations. But they won't unless you ask. Don't be bashful about seeking both information and assistance.

Perhaps the most reliable source of information of all, however, will be your own observations. Pay attention to what your "problem" is doing. When is it happening? Does it appear to be connected to anything else that is going on in the work environment or the employee's life? Do there appear to be "triggering" events for the problematical behavior? Your direct observations may teach you a lot. In the meantime, try to avoid making baseless assumptions. They may be way off the mark. For example, the fact that the employee of your focus likes to heft a few beers on her own time does not mean that she is "difficult" because she is an alcoholic. She may or may not be. If she is, that may or may not be the source of the problem. You would be well-advised to keep digging until you are certain about exactly what is going on.

The employee himself may be your best source for identifying the root cause of the "difficult" behavior. This is the time to be open and honest in your approach. When in conversation you bring the unacceptable behavior to his attention, *ask* him what he believes is the source of the problem. He, of course, may vehemently deny that there is a problem. But you have lost nothing by asking. You will at least have learned that denial is a part of the problem. On the other hand, you may be surprised at receiving an honest response. Take the time to listen carefully, even if you do not agree with what he has to say. You are learning his side of the story which ultimately could prove helpful in resolving the difficulty. None of this has been a waste of time or effort.

There is at least one cardinal rule for dealing with problematical behavior by a "difficult" employee. Do not delay in confronting the behavior in hopes that it will get better. That is very unlikely to happen. The sooner you meet the issue head-on the sooner the chance for improved behavior to occur. Get on it.

Your research into the background of the "difficult" employee may tell you what, if anything, has been done in the past to address the issue. Is there any indication that something worked, even partially or temporarily? If so, it may be worth trying again, perhaps with modifications. If nothing has really worked at all, there would appear to be little value in applying precisely the same remedy that has been tried before without favorable results. Or maybe a half-hearted attempt at correction has been tried in the past in an effort lacking the degree of resolution that you can apply. In that case you may want to try again. You will have to be the judge of the likelihood of success this time. Whatever remedy is applied—counseling or discipline or both—will have to be done with your full attention and intent to resolve the problematical performance issue. That is just the way you do these things as the effective leader that you are.

Certainly, each difficulty and each "difficult" police employee is at least somewhat different from all the rest. Each may require a slightly different approach over a different time frame. You have by now figured out that there is no "universal size and fit" response to a given problem or its solution. But you also must know that there are certain problems that must be addressed immediately as soon as they come to your attention. Apparent violations of the criminal statutes by any employee must result in the immediate alteration of the employee's duty status followed by a prompt investigation of potential criminal offenses. Likewise, allegations of gender-based or racial/ethnic harassment or discrimination must result in the immediate notification of Human Resources authorities, protection of the alleged victim(s), and a thorough inquiry into the claimed misconduct. Alleged bullying of any citizen or colleague must receive the same prompt treatment. In each case, your quick notification of your agency's chain of command is mandatory. This extreme variety of "difficult" employee must be dealt with quickly and effectively if actual misconduct is established.

As a leader you most assuredly will be confronted by unique people producing unique challenges. How to deal with them effectively may be the greatest challenge of all. Determining just how to go about it will be your next decision-making point.

WHAT YOU CAN AND CAN'T DO

In the Neanderthal era of law enforcement when the sergeant had to be the toughest guy on the team the threat of a good thrashing may on occasion have been the chosen response to a problematical employee. It is safe to say that those days have passed. Given the removal of that dubious option, what *can* you do to correct the behavior of a "difficult" employee?

Actually, there are a number of things you can do. You should, however, be aware at the outset that there are also a number of less-than-helpful employee responses you may draw in reaction to your efforts. For example:

- The employee may pledge on the soul of his departed grandmother to do whatever is necessary to end the unacceptable behavior—and then do absolutely nothing.
- The individual may react emotionally with tears and expressions of despair, real or fake.
- The employee may flare into aggressive anger and attempt to back you down via intimidation.
- He or she may attempt to minimize the whole affair, characterizing it as overblown.
- The employee may refuse to talk to you at all, claiming persecution and unfair treatment.
- The individual might deny that a problem exists in spite of solid evidence to the contrary.
- He or she may blame the whole problem on a misunderstanding or "personality conflict" between him and the source of the complaint.

Or the problem employee may respond by using each and every one of these red herring tactics in one way or another. Or his response may be something entirely different. (One seriously troubled police employee turned her chair and her back to the supervisor and refused to acknowledge his presence.) Regardless of the employee response you elicit, your priority remains unchanged: secure a change in behavior by the offending employee in lieu of very serious repercussions. At the far end of the scale lies termination from employment. If this is a real possibility, it is both acceptable and desirable to let the employee know that. In the process you should not permit to go unchallenged unacceptable behavior directed at you, the supervisor. Insubordination in any form is not something that can be tolerated.

On the other hand, the individual may surprise you with apparent sincerity in agreeing that there is a problem and expressing a personal willingness to solve it. It really can work out that way. If it does, your task has just gotten a lot easier. Realize, however, that your employee may be sincere or putting on an award-worthy piece of acting. The proof will be in the pudding, as the old expression goes.

Before you launch your effort to help your troubled employee towards a successful resolution of his troubling behavior you need to know what you can and can't do on the way to a positive outcome. You must first be cognizant of laws or organizational rules and policies that set parameters for your actions. Confer with your agency's legal advisor or HR specialists for guidance if you have any doubts at all about the limits of your authority. It is preferable to get advice *before* you stray beyond the limits of what you are allowed to do and end up having to make amends. Once again, keep your chain of command advised of your plans and actions.

It may be helpful to examine the personnel records and talk to the employee's previous supervisors about what remedies may have been tried previously and what may have helped improve behavior to some degree. You also need to know what definitely did not work. It is not out of bounds for you to ask the employee what he thinks would help resolve the problem. Again, he may deny the existence of a problem entirely or say he doesn't know what would work. Nothing is lost in the attempt, however. He just might voice an idea worth trying.

It is unlikely that there exists a single "magic" formula that will solve the problems brought about by a "difficult" employee. Absent the existence of such a formula you should feel free to be innovative—within reason—in solving the difficulty. After all, if you are the one held accountable for helping find a solution then you have earned the right to some leeway in your actions. Once more, it is a good idea to seek suggestions from your colleagues who may have encountered a similar challenge. You may even know successful leaders outside your organization with whom you feel comfortable discussing the situation you are facing, all within the appropriate limitations on releasing confidential personnel information.

If the problem you are confronting is a very serious one (example: an alleged criminal act) your means for dealing with it may be dictated by your employer's formal disciplinary procedures. Your obligation, of course, is to follow them to the letter. But many "difficult" employees have not engaged in misconduct to that extreme. In these situations, you often can rely upon tactics and techniques you learned through your study of employee counseling and discipline guidelines. These guideposts may include the following advice:

Know your facts. Be sure that the information of inappropriate conduct that you are acting on is correct and complete. If you do not have all the facts straight, delay confronting the "difficult" employee until you are clear on what has supposedly occurred. Do not allow this to result in a major delay in your taking action, but do be comfortable that you have your facts straight before you act.

Seek a private place and time. Correcting out-of-line employee behavior is not a spectator sport. Nor is it something that you want to rush through. Plan for privacy and sufficient, unrushed time for the discussion with your employee. You want to do this right, not quickly. Your employee needs to have the time to tell his side of the story if he elects to do so. At the same time, it should be clear that you are in charge of the meeting and will control the agenda.

Don't beat around the bush. The "difficult" employee most likely knows the purpose of the meeting. It won't be helpful to waste time talking about the weather or last night's ball game. Get to the purpose of the meeting straight away. Softening the complaint won't be helpful, either. Lay out what's wrong as directly and clearly as possible. Strive not to come across as hesitant, uncomfortable, or unsure of yourself.

Control your emotions. Particularly if you have had to address the same issue previously with the same employee, it may be easy to express frustration and outright anger with the offender. Within reason, honest frustration is appropriate. Otherwise, do your best to keep all of your emotions in check. If some version of appeal or grievance process results from the meeting you do not want to arm your employee with a legitimate claim that he was "bullied" or otherwise intimidated by his boss. Stay calm but be direct.

Listen but don't be diverted. Your troubled employee deserves the right to tell his side of the story. Hear him out. Then bring the conversation back to the problem and what has to be done to fix it. It is important not to be sidetracked into talking at length about past grievances or episodes in which the employee felt he was mistreated. Stay on task.

Offer your help. By the close of the meeting it must be made clear to the employee that he is the one responsible for correcting the unacceptable behavior, and no one else. That said, it is also appropriate to offer your help and advice along the way. You might, for instance, offer to alert him anytime you see any indication that he is about to relapse into inappropriate conduct. You also can make references for professional help, such as a counselor or police psychologist, if you feel that is appropriate for the problem behavior.

Spell out exactly what you expect. By the close of your session with the problematical employee he should be left with no doubt about what he is expected to do. (He very likely knew that going into the meeting.) State it very clearly and then ask if he understands what is expected. Agreement is not required; understanding is. Repeat yourself if necessary.

Make it clear what will happen if the problem persists. Your employee needs to know what the consequences will be if he fails to produce the desired change in performance. Again, spell it out clearly and directly. Your next step should be to assure that the promised consequences actually occur if the needed change does not take place. Keep your own boss up to date on what has happened so far.

Follow-up to determine if lasting change takes place. Your employee may or may not have the best intentions of changing his unacceptable conduct, whatever it happens to be. The question is whether or not he will make the required change. The second is whether or not the change will continue over time. You only will know the answer by careful and continuing observation of his behavior. He should be made aware that you are observing. It is also perfectly fine for you to give him progress reports, including praise when he is doing it the right way and correction if he isn't. If progress does not continue it will be time for serious corrective measures, including the possibility of termination.

Document in detail. If it's not written down, it didn't happen. You have heard that many times before. Whether it is an exaggeration or not, the truth is that it will be hard either to reward or punish what your employee is doing without a written record to serve as backing for future personnel action. The fact that you are recording everything in writing should not be kept secret from the employee, either.

You can and should offer the "difficult" employee both understanding and empathy. But you also must make good on your promise of consequences if the called-for course correction does not occur—and continue. Never be hesitant to implement deserved discipline for unacceptable job performance, even if that discipline ultimately results in termination. Your other employees are watching and will not be impressed by a boss who growls but never bites, even when that response is richly deserved. It is important that everyone knows what is and isn't acceptable behavior and what the consequences are for intentionally inappropriate conduct.

When it comes to your employee audience, education is the goal you are seeking. But there is another, equally important target in your sights. . . .

THE GOAL YOU BOTH SEEK

Change for the better. That's what you are after. Hopefully, that is what your employee is seeking, too. Regardless of his or her objective, this is what will need to happen to satisfy you and your organization. You are not seeking temporary or partial change, either. A consistent, complete, lasting alteration from unacceptable behavior is what you expect and must have. Nothing short of that will suffice. You should not have to intervene again because the improper conduct has resurfaced.

There is more. You also are seeking a return to a positive work environment for the other members of the team. And beyond that, you need to see improved service to the citizen-customers that you all are paid to serve. It may sound trite, but in the final analysis they are why each of you has a job.

Because you are the kind of caring supervisor that you are you are doubtlessly hoping that your "difficult" employee gets as much satisfaction out of his or her improved performance as you do. You want your employee to be productive but you also hope for him to be at least reasonably content at work. You earnestly desire a positive employee-supervisor relationship that does not include verbal sniping by either party. You want your boss to notice the solution of a problem that you and your employee, working together, have achieved.

All of these good things are certainly possible and absolutely desirable. With the effort you have put into it there is a good chance that things will work out exactly that way.

But they might not. In the real world that you and your employee inhabit success will not be achieved every time. You will not oversee the successful transformation of every problematical police employee that you ever encounter. It may be difficult indeed to achieve a radical change in behavior in an employee who has been "difficult" for a very long time. All you can offer is your best. That's what you always do.

It is important that you remember that it is the "difficult" employee who bears 100% of the responsibility for solving the problem or problems that brought the two of you face-to-face in the first place. You can help. You can advise and counsel. You can set out the requirements for change in a crystal-clear fashion and be prepared to enforce consequences if required change does not occur. But again: the responsibility for fixing the problem remains with the one who caused it. It is not your fault if the required change fails to occur. It is important that you remember that.

SUMMARY

The problem employee, left to his or her own designs, can severely damage an organization. He or she literally can transform coming to work into an experience to be dreaded by colleagues and supervisors alike. The problem employee can be that destructive.

As a strong leader you almost certainly will deal with problem employees throughout your leadership career. You will do it effectively because of the sort of skilled and courageous leader you are. You will be able to identify the problem employee and recognize his tactics for avoiding correction. You have learned your own tactics for responding to problematic behavior and correcting it and you will rely on them when confronting the problematic police employee.

In the most positive scenario, you and the problem employee are able to reach a solution acceptable to you both. The solution results in positive behavior or favorable job performance change on a continuing basis. That, of course, is the arrangement you are seeking. But you are also now equipped to deal with the problem employee who simply doesn't admit the existence of a problem, or express a sincere desire to solve it. With or without the employee's help, you will pursue a long-lasting solution that is beneficial to all concerned—even the problem employee himself. That, too, is within your abilities as an effective leader.

Problem-solving is what you do as a leader. Sometimes the problem confronting you will have a face and a name. With courage, leadership skills, and empathy you will solve that problem, too.

Chapter 13

RESPONDING TO THE UNHAPPY CITIZEN

It has probably happened to you. You have visited a business establishment or government agency to ask a question or make a complaint and left (after considerable frustration) with the impression that you are the one who doesn't know what he is doing or, worse, has done something wrong. The exasperating turns along the way may have included disinterested (at best) or semi-hostile (at worst) employees who were not hesitant to indicate by their words, actions, or both that you were rudely interfering with something more important that they were doing. Something like texting, gossiping, or surfing the Net.

If you have attempted to phone in your inquiry or complaint you may have found yourself transferred from one extension to another while listening to really bad music or a propaganda (advertising) recording, only to end up parked at last on the voicemail of someone who has just gone on an extended sabbatical to Bora-Bora. If you were not angry when you started this hopeless trek, you likely are by now. Welcome to what passes for the land of openness and transparency, at least in some quarters. Or at least that's what the outfit's mission statement tells you that you'll find when you venture there.

You are probably thinking by now that this is certainly not the reception citizens receive when they contact *my* organization with a question or complaint. Hopefully you are correct in your assumption. But it should not surprise you to learn that because of their previous experiences, hopefully elsewhere, that is precisely the reception too many of your citizen-customers *think* they will get when they contact your organization with a question or beef of some kind. As a good leader, you will want to do everything you can to dispel that perception and instead leave your citizen with the feeling that he or she has been heard with empathy and courtesy, and that something positive will happen as a result of the interaction. This chapter will aid you in accomplishing that laudable goal.

HEARING HIM OUT

Unless you have led a pleasantly untypical life, you doubtlessly have made a complaint before, whether it was to a cell phone provider, auto dealer, or government bureaucrat. You may recall being cut off before you finished your tale of woe, or perhaps being figuratively patted on the head and basically told to run along. Equally doubtlessly, you remember the bitter taste the whole experience left with you.

As an ethical and empathetic leader in your law enforcement agency you have determined long before now that the just-described scenario is not one you want to create with your own citizen-complainant. There are several positive steps you can take to keep that from happening. Consider the following advice:

- Try to avoid assumptions and foregone conclusions. It is very easy to assume that you have heard it all and the present complainant will have nothing to say that you have not heard before. It is easy to decide in advance that the lady wanting to talk to you about the "rudeness" of one of your officers just wants to get out of the ticket she received. In reality, that may not be her mission at all. She actually may have information that you need regarding the performance of one of your people. But you won't know unless you approach the conversation with an open mind without pre-drawn conclusions. To quote a veteran Internal Affairs sergeant: "I used to approach these things with the feeling 'that's impossible.' I don't say that anymore." There is a lesson for you here.
- Let him tell his story without interruption. You will recall how you felt when someone interrupted you repeatedly as you tried to make an inquiry or lodge a complaint. The person standing across from you or at the other end of the telephone is unlikely to feel any differently if you repeatedly interrupt or challenge his or her version of events. It is perfectly alright to nod from

time to time to indicate that he should continue. This is sometimes called "full face" listening. That means that you are fully focused on the speaker without making faces, sounds, or gestures that telegraph you are impatient or disinterested. An unhappy citizen who has been allowed to vent fully is oftentimes easier to deal with afterwards. It is always worth a try.

- When he's done, ask questions and clarify. Once the complainant has finished it is both permissible and advisable to seek clarification of any parts of his story you do not understand. You can seek additional information at this point, too. Endeavor not to come across as aggressively challenging his version of events. Let him know that you are asking the questions so that you can appropriately follow-up on his concerns.

- Continue to watch your demeanor and body language. This is not the time or place for grimaces, eye rolls, or any other theatrics that indicate you abhor the whole process that you are currently involved in, or doubt the veracity and parentage of the complainant. Your job is to project the image of the unbiased, caring professional that you really are. Be alert to what the rest of your body is doing, too. This is not the spot for crossed arms or a tapping foot that betray your true feelings. It is possible, of course, to show the same feelings through your voice to a complainant at the other end of the phone line. Be careful of what you say and how you say it. It is worth remembering, too, that in today's electronics-saturated world there is a good chance that you are being recorded by your caller. You always want to come across as the professional that you really are.

- Apologize, if appropriate. It is sometimes called the lawyer's prime directive: never apologize, never admit doing anything wrong. And it's not always the best advice. You will have to be the judge of that. It is also possible to explain and defend your employees' actions or words and still apologize that your complainant was upset by what happened. It is OK to say that you *understand* the individual's reaction. People are frequently shocked to get an apology from a government employee, most especially one who wears a badge. The apology itself, if you believe it is merited, may in itself be enough to defuse a complaint and calm a confused or unhappy citizen-customer. Keep it available in your leader's toolbox.

- Tell them what happens next. It's what you would want to know if you were the inquiring or complaining party. If you are planning to talk with the police personnel involved to get more details, let the citizen know that. If you need to do some further investigation (almost certainly you will) let him know that, too. If a complaint is going to be forwarded for a formal investigation, make him aware of that, as well. Let your citizen know what the time frame to get all of this done may be. If he is expecting a next-day resolution and doesn't get it, he may be upset all over again. If you are the one who will be doing the follow-up and contacting him again, let him know when to expect to hear from you. Then, be sure you keep your promise within the time frame that you have indicated. Doing that without fail is vital for maintaining your personal credibility as well as that of your agency. Know that you may receive phone calls requesting a progress report. Answer the calls with patience and timeliness. Again, it is your personal reputation for believability that is at stake.

WHAT ARE THE HOT BUTTONS?

There are things that you most certainly do not want to hear when you call a government agency to ask a question or make a complaint. (Refer to the chapter on customer service!) You do not want to be told that the whole thing is your fault, "it isn't our policy", or some other version of a "kiss-off." You don't want to be parked on eternal hold or transferred to an unattended voicemail box. And you certainly do not want to be left with the impression that your issue is apparently a great bother and an imposition to the organization that you have called. *It is fair to assume that the citizen-customer doesn't want any of that, either.*

Be aware that your attitude is showing throughout the inquiry or complaint process. Try hard to keep it positive and nonjudgmental. You want to be seen the same way in which your organization wishes to be labelled: honestly caring, open, and accessible. Apply the same problem-solving techniques that you rely on in your provision of exceptional customer service. Techniques such as:

- Treat people as individuals and use their name.
- Maintain good eye contact and an open (not threatening) posture during an in-person meeting.
- Listen carefully; avoid the temptation to cut off the speaker and commence solving (or denying) his concern.
- Allow him to save face, if possible. If he has made a mistake it is not necessary to rub his face in it.
- Seek agreement on something, even if it is just that it's a beautiful day.
- Stay calm and in control. Try to avoid raising your voice, even if he raises his. Take some deep, calming breaths if you find yourself overheating.
- Try to build trust with the individual by demonstrating patience, courtesy, tact, and credibility.
- Thank him for bringing his concerns to your attention, even if you may be feeling less than thankful at the moment.
- Stress what you and your agency can do for him, not what you cannot.
- Tell the truth; do not promise something that you cannot deliver. But keep any promises that you do make.
- Try hard to ignore angry, exaggerated, or rude comments made by a complainant. He likely is attacking the situation, not you personally.
- Smile when appropriate. Nod affirmatively from time to time to indicate that it is alright to continue speaking.
- Attempt to show as much empathy as is appropriate in the situation. You can lament his difficulty or confusion without taking responsibility for it. It costs nothing and may help defuse an angry and frustrated complainant.

Through your patient listening you may be able to calm and at least partially satisfy an initially confused and perhaps highly upset citizen. Law enforcement leaders just like you have accomplished just that many times before.

One of your goals is to handle the situation at your level and keep the higher brass from having to get involved. But realize that things will not always work out that way. When it does not, you have by no means "failed." It's not your fault. Some folks simply want to talk to the "Big Dog" and no one else, whether that is a realistic expectation or not. Also know that there are things that your bosses need to be notified of right away. Allegations of significant employee misconduct are among them. The decision may be made to take the following inquiry or investigation out of your hands to be continued elsewhere, such as in Internal Affairs. That decision cannot be made unless you promptly notify the appropriate people.

It is also possible that the individual you thought you had satisfied today may rethink the whole thing tomorrow and decide that he wants to go higher. That is his right. Again, you have not failed in your responsibilities. As long as you know you have done your earnest best in addressing his issues you have nothing to be ashamed of. You are simply experiencing the vagaries of human nature. Just keep doing what you have been doing well and move forward.

As you know by now, sometimes there is a grain of truth to be found in even the most outlandish-sounding complaint. Other times the truth will be found somewhere in between the poles-apart versions related by the individual actors in the drama. Yet other times the citizen's complaint is totally accurate or absolutely a constructed falsehood. You won't know for sure until you have engaged in the effort of some unbiased fact-finding.

If the complaint is one of employee misconduct you will, of course, want to get the police employee's version of events plus the observations of any witnesses to the affair. What evidence exists, documentary or otherwise, that may shed light on what transpired? Are there body camera images? Meanwhile, do your very best to put behind you any preconceived notions of what happened. You just might be very mistaken. Do not rush unnecessarily in your fact-finding, either. It is far more important to be thorough and accurate than fast. Do not hesitate to re-contact the complainant to flesh out details or answer additional questions that your inquiry may have brought up.

Your agency will have its own policies and procedures for responding to citizen complaints and allegations of police employee misconduct. Be sure you follow them to the letter. Keep your chain of command briefed on what you have learned if your citizen contact has resulted in an allegation of official misconduct. Let them know what you are doing about it. Doing so helps both you and your bosses by letting them know what is going on if your complainant suddenly decides to "take it upstairs," such as to an elected official or the news media. If that's what he chooses to do, so be it. You just don't want your agency head to be caught off guard by the escalation.

If what you have learned from a citizen amounts to an allegation of possible criminal conduct (rape, assault, robbery, etc.) another line has just been crossed. It most probably will be time to turn the complaint over to Professional Standards and/or criminal investigators to take it from there. It likely will be necessary for the accused employee, who should still be considered innocent until proven otherwise, to be advised of his rights before the conversation proceeds. Put your own inquiry on hold, advise your chain of command, and await instructions before proceeding on your own.

In the majority of inquiries and complaints that you will handle there will be no allegation of actual criminal misconduct. In these situations you will be free to pursue your own fact-finding efforts. Complete your research for any documentary or other evidence. Check your department's records to see if this complainant has made similar allegations in the past. If so, what was the finding of the inquiry conducted at that time? Obviously, a prior "record" on the part of either the citizen or the employee is not proof of what happened this time. But it is helpful information to have as you dig deeper.

Often more important than what you learn from others is what you glean from the police employee or employees at the heart of the incident. Your contact with your employee should be done privately and in a non-accusatory manner. Simply relate to him or her what you know so far: Mr. X asked or complained about Y and you need to know what happened in order to respond to him. Let your employee know as soon as you know if a formal investigation is to be conducted, and, if so, who will be doing it. If you are just gathering information to answer a citizen's questions, tell him that, too.

Keep the conversation as informal as possible unless what you learn tells you that the whole affair demands a Professional Standards investigation. Let your employee know that you will be getting back in touch with the inquiring citizen and telling him what you have learned. Assure your employee that you will be sticking up for him if he has done nothing wrong. If he acknowledges an error on his part, let him know that you will so advise the citizen and offer an apology on his behalf, if that appears the appropriate response. If you are contemplating some kind of corrective action for your subordinate, let him know that, too. The idea is to be as open as possible with everyone involved, accuser and accused alike. If you have determined the situation to be more misunderstanding than misconduct, so much the better. Experience has shown that an honest and patient explanation will satisfy many if not most puzzled and perhaps miffed citizens.

RESOLVING THE ISSUE

You have now determined to your satisfaction what happened and why. If you have confirmed that your organization or one or more of its employees erred, you have decided (or shortly will have decided) what to do about it. You now must get back to your citizen-complainant or questioner with a response.

Perhaps you already know the answer from your previous contact with the individual: What does he want to have happen as a result of his question or complaint, assuming for present purposes that the agency or one of its people messed up? If you don't know, now is the time to ask just that. Does he want the problem to be fixed? (Probably.) Does he expect an apology? (It certainly wouldn't hurt.) Both of the preceding? Or what? You may need to ask the question directly to find out. Then, let your questioner-complainant know what you are actually going to do. If you plan to correct an errant employee, it is permissible to say so without divulging specifics. Tell the truth, even if the individual relates that he feels your response is insufficient. You are trying to avoid an "appeal" of your handling of the situation. If he wants to talk to someone "higher up" anyway, courteously let him know how to go about it. Then, promptly advise those "higher ups" what may be coming their way. Let them know the essential facts of the case and what you have done in an attempt to resolve the situation. Once more, remember: you have not failed. It is every citizen's right to disagree with "official" findings. At some point you may have done that yourself!

The involved police employees also need to know how the whole affair concluded. If they have done nothing wrong, they need to know that. Perhaps their extreme patience or smart tactics need recognized. If the situation could have been handled better, such as more effort being put into explaining what the police were doing and why, your people need to hear that, too.

Follow your agency's established procedures for documenting the details of the inquiry or complaint and your handling of it. Some departments may require extensive documentation while others expect little or none. Keep things as informal as you can for everybody's benefit. It is one more thing you can do to be considerate to everyone concerned.

As a leader you are good at resolving problems, complaints and questions included. It's what you do. As with the rest of your many responsibilities, do your best but realize that you will not make everyone happy all the time. Realize that there are people out there who will never be satisfied no matter what you do or say. It is always worth extending your very best efforts but it is unlikely that you will alter their basic nature in the short time you have to spend with them. Again, be satisfied that you have done your best.

Life and work always will present you with unhappy people on occasion. Fortunately, even in your chosen profession of law enforcement dedicated-unhappy human beings will be in the minority of those you deal with. Your ethics and your empathetic nature will dictate that you will always try your best to solve the hurts, real or exaggerated, of unhappy people. Patience, tact, self-confidence, and empathy will be foremost among your tools for accomplishing that worthy goal. That's just who you are.

SUMMARY

One of your jobs as a leader is to receive the questions and complaints of confused or angry citizens and attempt to resolve their issues. Much of the time you will succeed to one degree or another in doing just that. You will accomplish it by recalling the times that you have had questions or complaints and how you were treated for good or ill by those who responded to you—or failed to do so. As in so many of your endeavors, you will try really hard to treat these people better than you may have been treated when you were in their shoes.

You will achieve this improved state of affairs by utilizing patience, tact, and superior listening skills. You will steer clear of foregone conclusions and permit an angry or frustrated customer to vent without responding with anger or personal attack. You will remember that cops do make mistakes, even if they are unintentional ones, on occasion. You will show genuine empathy and even offer an apology if one is needed. But you also will be honest enough to so advise a complaining party if a diligent investigation reveals that he or she was not wronged. Realizing that complaints sometimes emanate from simple misunderstandings and miscommunications, you will go out of your way to explain why cops do what they do, and how legitimate procedures may on occasion be mistaken for improper police conduct. If a mistake *has* been made, you will do your best to correct it and assure that it does not happen again.

It is in everyone's best interest that your citizen-customers receive the exceptional police service that they are paying for. Anytime your investigation reveals that errors have been made through police policies, procedures, or personnel you will endeavor to correct them, at whatever level in the organization that must take place. Just as important, you will see to it that everyone directly involved knows what is being done, and how soon it will be accomplished. That amounts to serving in your important role of a clear and credible communicator. And that is a role you can fulfill very well indeed.

Chapter 14

LEADING YOUR PEOPLE TO EXCEPTIONAL CUSTOMER SERVICE

Everyone has his or her own horror story about nightmarish customer service received at the hands of an apparently uncaring, officious, unpleasant employee. These customer service disasters have taken place at airline ticket counters, offices of medical providers, and "service" desks in a hundred different varieties of commercial establishments. Oftentimes they have occurred when a desperate customer seeking assistance has telephoned for help and ended up ensnared in the hopeless web of a megafirm's telephone boiler room operation, located somewhere "offshore" and staffed by souls universally named "Dan" or "Diane."

It will not shock you to hear that far too often government agencies and government employees are labelled as among the worst offenders in providing sub-standard customer care, or virtually no care at all. Law enforcement agencies are sometimes mentioned in these lists of "poor service providers." One big city police chief admitted feeling apprehensive and a little bit intimidated when, out of uniform and unidentified, he approached the front desk of the police station in a neighboring city to request service. Sadly, his apprehensions proved justified when he was "serviced" by an evidently-bored, discourteous desk officer. The chief was left wondering, "Do my people treat citizens that way?"

Fortunately, there is another, brighter side to the customer service scene. If you'll think about it, you probably will call instances where service providers went above and beyond to assist you in solving a particularly vexing problem. Those problem-solving people are out there, too, and if you are fortunate you may have met a number of them over your years. These are the folks about whom you may have said to yourself, "I wish they were part of *my* organization."

Law enforcement is full of stories of police people who have done amazing things in the name of customer service. Their feats range from the kitten in the tree rescue to the cop who mowed the little old lady's lawn for her, and a thousand stories in-between. There are a lot of legitimate customer service heroes out there, but this one may take the cake:

A Patrol division chief in a mid-sized American police department was working in his office one snowy afternoon when he fielded a call from a near-panicked assistant city manager. She had called the police chief, who was unavailable, the watch commander, Internal Affairs, and the city's Public Works Department. No one could or would help her. It seems she had received a telephone call from an irate citizen who complained that during a traffic stop in front of her house the preceding night the department's officers had permitted the female teenaged occupants of the stopped vehicle to squat down out of sight between parked vehicles and empty their over-filled bladders. But that wasn't the heart of the complaint. One young woman had deposited a used sanitary napkin on the street, and the indignant caller wanted it removed by the City, post-haste. The flustered assistant manager was at her wits' end in trying to get someone to help her accomplish this extraordinary citizen demand.

As a good leader, there are probably things that you just don't ask your people to do. Apparently, the division chief felt the same way. He gathered up some disposable gloves, a paper sack, the keys to a patrol vehicle and drove to the address of the reported travesty. He arrived only to find that the address where the stop occurred was actually at least a city block into the neighboring city. Undeterred, he knocked at the door of the complainant's house, hoping to get some help in locating the offending item. The man who opened the door spoke no English and looked as though he believed the officer was there to take him away. He was no help. Still unfazed, the chief began scraping the newly-fallen snow at the curbside until he finally located his target. He then discovered that the subject of his quest was now frozen to the pavement. Still undeterred, he returned to his vehicle, obtained an ice scraper, and chipped away at the mess until he could retrieve and bag it. Mission accomplished, the chief returned to the office, called the assistant city manager to let her know that the problem was solved, and never said another word about it to anyone. Until now.

None of this is to say that you must grub frozen sanitary napkins out of the gutter in order to be deserving of a reputation for providing exceptional customer service. You almost certainly enjoy that reputation already as a result of all the other things that you do. In addition, as a leader you are responsible for creating an atmosphere in which your subordinates share your belief in exceptional customer service and seek to deliver it to your constituents. The remainder of this chapter will offer you tips for securing outstanding customer service from the personnel you lead.

WHAT YOUR CITIZEN-CUSTOMERS WANT

Your citizens generally do not summon law enforcement because they are having an uneventful, pleasant day. Most often they are calling for help because they are confused, frightened, angry or otherwise upset about *something*. They want and need competent, effective, efficient assistance. Sometimes all they really seek is a patient, empathetic listener to hear their plight and offer some advice or reassurance. And that's where your people come in.

There are enterprises in existence that have excellent reputations for giving people not only what they want but more than they expected. Disney, Chick-fil-A, and Southwest Airlines are often mentioned as among them. There are many others. Private businesses having the best reputations for exceptional customer service oftentimes provide their employees some specific, simple guidelines for furnishing excellent customer service. They require that their people remember that:

- Customers are individuals with names, personal stories, and feelings.
- Customers are the reason each of us has a job.
- Customers are not interruptions to our work; they are our work.
- Our most important task is to take care of our customers.

There almost certainly are law enforcement officers who, for whatever reason or no reason at all, do not accept any of that. If so, they are wrong. It is not required that you change their beliefs. But it is your responsibility to see to that it that their beliefs do not prevent them from delivering exceptional service to the citizens they have promised to serve.

Whether he is approaching the counter in a hardware store or in your police station, a customer is reasonably expecting some of the same things:

Responsiveness. Someone will understand my predicament and offer some kind of timely assistance.

Reliability. The answer I am given or the action that is taken will address my situation, whatever it happens to be, appropriately and with results to the extent feasible.

Respect. The person I am working with understands my concerns and is psychologically supportive of me.

Reassurance. The person I am talking with has assured me that the worst is over or soon will be and it is going to alright.

None of these expectations is unreasonable. You expect the same when you are in your customer mode. You must emphasize the importance of these customer service guideposts to your police employees, sworn and nonsworn. They are the gatekeepers who will do much to establish the reputation of your entire agency, for good or ill.

Cops are practical people, so let them know that there are tangible, practical benefits for them beyond the opportunity to make someone feel better and feel good themselves. Satisfied customers can mean additional support for the police agency and its employees. Support that might be seen in additional personnel, vehicles, facilities, salaries, and other benefits.

No, neither you nor your people will succeed every time in turning an angry or frustrated citizen into a full-fledged police supporter. That's just life in the real world that you all inhabit. But it can happen often enough to make the whole effort worthwhile. More important than that, it is the right thing to do.

AVOIDING THE CUSTOMER SERVICE PITFALLS

Just as there are proven ways to deliver exceptional customer service, so, too, are there equally reliable ways to send it straight down the tubes. When one listens to the complaints of customers who feel they have been "serviced" rather than served, certain themes become evident. You may have had similar experiences as a customer. Some of the most often-heard negative comments include the following:

"Nobody listened to me."
"I was made to feel it was *my* fault."
"No one got back to me."
"The person I talked with was just plain rude."
"They rushed through the whole thing."
"The guy I talked with acted disinterested and bored."
"They said they couldn't help me. I was hoping they'd at least *try*."

None of these comments would appear to identify a customer who is happy about his or her interaction with a service provider. You may have made similar comments yourself after a failed attempt at gaining some customer service.

Why do these bad things happen to customers? Surely the "guilty" service providers do not start out with the goal of providing poor customer service. There can be a number influencing factors that can result in the delivery of poor customer service across a broad spectrum of vocations and professions, including yours. Factors such as:

Perceived lack of time to do it right. Overburdened employees rushing from one task or customer to the next seldom do a good or thorough job for any of those tasks or customers. Assigning too few people resources to customer service can lead to big mistakes, big trouble, and overall poor service.

Employees who have "heard it all before." This is an attitude problem most often demonstrated by personnel who simply would rather be doing something else—or nothing at all.

Employees who have a "disinterested" demeanor or who come across as impatient, authoritarian, and tactless. Once more, the supervisor of this employee has an "attitude" problem to address. The reasons behind the attitude could be endless.

Lack of resources. Whether it is due to an inadequate number of telephone lines, chairs, space, or employees, poor service can be the ultimate outcome of attempting to provide customer service with insufficient resources. Inadequate budgets obviously can play a role.

Inadequately qualified and/or trained employees. The best-intentioned employee cannot provide adequate customer service if he or she does not have appropriate knowledge, skills, and abilities to perform the job function. This is the fault of the organization, not the employee.

Overly-restrictive or confusing policies and procedures. Law enforcement agencies maintain binder after binder and disk after disk of rules, regulations, policies, and procedures. On occasion these voluminous guidelines are hopelessly complex, confusing, or out-of-date and keep an employee who wants to help a citizen-customer from doing so. The frontline employees who work under these guidelines often are the best judges of which provisions help and which actually make their job of helping customers harder. The pertinent guidelines are worth a look from time to time and revisions made where needed.

But of all the exceptional customer service obstacles, none is more detrimental to your organization and the people it serves than is the employee who displays an apparent attitude of studied indifference. As a leader, it is your responsibility to deal with this individual and the problems that he or she can promulgate. There are some effective steps you can take in addressing that problem.

DOING IT THE RIGHT WAY

Your very first step in leading your people to provide exceptional customer service is to serve as an excellent role model for your troops to see and hear in action. You have heard that many times before, but it is no less true in the vital area of customer service than in any of the other responsibilities you ably handle. That need for excellent example-setting applies to both your internal and external customers. Your subordinates, of course, must be counted among your internal customers. If you do not reliably attend to their needs and concerns in a responsible and timely manner, it is unlikely that you will find *them* anxious to serve their customers with their best efforts.

Your employees also are paying close attention to how you treat your department's citizen-customers. If you are rude to them or ridicule their personal issues or "ignorance" out of their presence you again should not be surprised if your subordinates do the same with their own customers. Know that you and your actions are always on display, especially to your own people. Endeavor to do it the right way every time.

Beyond your duties in serving as an excellent role model you are responsible for helping repair the shortcomings of an employee who is not fulfilling his obligations as a provider of good customer service. It wouldn't be surprising if you were already focused on this employee for other deficits in performance. It would be unusual if an employee providing less-than-sterling customer service was not displaying other performance issues, as well.

Your approach to this individual's customer service issues should not be greatly dissimilar from the manner in which you confront other employee shortcomings. Be direct; don't mince words. Present him with the complaint or your own observations regarding his customer service skills. Listen to his excuses or explanations, but don't back off. Make sure he understands what the problem is and what you expect to be done about it. Let your guy know that you both hope and expect to see improvement. Let him know as well that you will acknowledge any and all good work you see. Then, follow-up and keep watching for the change in performance that you must have. Award praise for any continuing improvement that you observe. Watch to see that it continues. If you fail to detect the results you expect, do not hesitate to bring that to his attention, as well. He needs to know that you are not going away until you see the lasting change that you have called for.

It also is worth the effort to again let all of your subordinates—not just the problematical one(s)—know the potential reward for treating their citizen-customers well: more tangible support for them from constituents who are telling their elected officials about the good work their cops are doing. What they are doing is really no more than community-oriented policing on steroids. After all, one of the most important components of any COP program is caring customer service.

SUMMARY

You consistently provide exceptional customer service to the people you are sworn to serve and protect. That is a given. Your goal and the logical next step is to elicit that same kind of exceptional service from your subordinates. You accomplish that by once again serving as an excellent role model. You do it by clearly stating your customer service expectations for your crew. You do it by monitoring their interactions with the public and then praising or correcting, as appropriate. You also let your people know the tangible benefits that can accrue to them through the provision of exceptional service.

From personal experience you know what exceptional customer service looks, sounds, and feels like. Your have learned from experiencing the "other kind," too. That's not the kind you and your employees want to deliver. Being the leader that you are, you will not let that happen.

In all of your dealings with the rest of the world, you want to get your money's worth. So do your citizen-customers. In leading your people to provide extraordinary customer service to the community you will be assuring that your taxpayers will be getting the excellent customer service they expect and deserve. You and your corps of professionals can take pride in yet another job well done.

Chapter 15

BECOMING MR. MICROPHONE:
HANDLING THE MEDIA SUCCESSFULLY

You have heard it time and again: as a leader, you are the face of your organization. It's true, and nowhere is it more accurate than in your relationship with the representatives of the news media.

In today's world dominated by the influence of the mass media your citizens often view their public servants through the camera lenses of the electronic media. That's not to say that the print media (newspapers and magazines) do not still have a major influence on public thinking and opinion. They do. But more and more the latest generations get most of their news and form most of their opinions from what they receive over their smartphone or see and hear displayed on the big screen in their home. If you and your agency have a message to get out and an image you want to project, you will have to make use of these elements of the media to the fullest extent possible. You will be required to utilize the media to reach your public safety consumers with the information they need to stay safe. You will need the media to tell your taxpayers about the good work their officers are doing. You will require the media's help to project the positive images of your cops you want the public to see.

At the same time, the media need you to satisfy their audience's hunger for news on crimes, disasters, scandals, and other happenings in the local community. They can and will still do their job of newsgathering without your help, but your lack of cooperation will make the task more difficult. That makes it less likely that the newsgatherers will treat you favorably when they report what they gather—without your help—as the facts. That is not in your best interest. Cooperation, at least to a reasonable degree, is a good thing.

There is no denying that past relations between the news media and the law enforcement community have not always been peachy. In a few locales and among a few professionals on both sides that atmosphere of mutual distrust remains today. That's not good for anyone, either. Not all that long ago the news reporter was likely to view the police officer (or flatfoot) as brutal, quick to believe in someone's guilt, biased against minorities, not too bright, clannish, and willing to lie wholesale to protect himself and his peers. The cops also had their own stereotypical view of a reporter. He or she was a left-wing, liberal, communist-sympathizing, bleeding heart who was always willing to make up lies to shield the guilty and pillory the hard-working cop. In that sort of atmosphere there were not a lot of cops and reporters who would confess to being good friends. And both sides suffered from the rampant mistrust.

The truth is that law enforcement and the media often attract some of the same kind of people to their ranks. These are (often young) persons who:

- Have a strong sense of justice
- Desire to stick up for the perceived underdog
- Are aggressive and not easily denied access
- Are a bit egotistical
- Are proud of their profession and what they do
- Tend to see themselves as misunderstood and mistreated.

In other words, law enforcement CEOs and news organization bosses are often seeking to hire the same Type AAA personalities. Little wonder that these alphas should sometimes clash on an incident scene!

The reality is that law enforcement and the media have much to offer each other. They need each other, to boot. Often, law enforcement has the information the media wants and needs. The news media hold the access to the public that law enforcement needs to disseminate the information they want placed in front of that public. Each side can benefit from cooperation with the other. Everybody can "win," at least most of the time.

As a leader you have a major role to play in all of this. By virtue of your leadership status it is you the reporters and camerapersons will seek out at a crime, accident, or incident scene. They will stick a camera or microphone in your face and ask you to comment knowingly on what is happening, what has just happened, and what will happen next. They may expect you to know all of this with very little advance notice. And, like you, they probably will be in a hurry to move on to the next crisis. There probably will be more than a little stress present.

How you respond to the ladies and gentlemen of the press will have very much to do with the image you project to the public for both yourself and your entire organization. Some of this you will accomplish through the media interviews that you give on-scene or elsewhere. Other times you will further positive police-media relations through the news releases you prepare on an event of media interest. But you will accomplish the most of all by the way in which you behave when interacting with the media representatives. It will be through your displayed integrity, credibility, and professionalism that you will impress these people the most and help build a positive working relationship between the media and your law enforcement agency. Yet again, you will find yourself on-stage as the positive role model of what a police leader (and a police spokesperson) should be. Indeed, you will be the face of your agency.

This chapter will help you successfully shepherd the minions of the media on the scene of a crime or other happening attracting significant media interest. It will offer some tips for giving a winning media interview, live or otherwise. It will arm you with guidelines for preparing an effective news release. Perhaps the most important of all, it will furnish you with some all-important rules to guide your personal and professional relations with the representatives of the news business.

You *can* work comfortably and effectively with the news media while you inform a public always anxious to know what their public safety professionals are doing. You can help protect that same public. You can do this and do it well. Here's how it's done.

YOUR NEWS MEDIA DUTIES ON-SCENE

As the man or woman in charge on a crime or incident scene you already have plenty to do. You are not really ecstatic to see THEM—the people with the cameras, notepads, and microphones—winding their way among the emergency vehicles to find YOU, the person they assume has all of the information they need. You probably would prefer that they find someone else to talk to. The department's Public Information Officer or an agency Brass Hat, for instance. However, it turns out that you are IT, at least for the time being. Welcome to the world of media relations! These media folks are counting on you, the person obviously in charge, to give them the full story, or at least enough of it to satisfy their bosses and deadlines. You have just become the image and voice of your agency.

In addition to responding to the needs of the media, you have your own people to satisfy on-scene. You want to set a good example for them in how a police professional should relate to the news media. Courtesy, professionalism, patience, and *reasonableness* should be your guidewords in working with the media. Once more, your intent must be to serve as an exceptional role model.

Reasonableness is the key to your on-scene media relations. Beyond the need to be courteous and accessible you should have a legitimate reason for the on-scene restrictions you place on the media. It is possible that well-intentioned officers have placed some fairly stringent limits on the press that do not make good sense to either you or the media reps. (One supervisor arrived on the scene of a supposed barricaded gunman to find the media penned a half-mile away while neighbors strolled within sight of the alleged offender's address.) You may need to make some quick alterations to the media access plan. If you do, notify your cops of the reasons behind your decision as soon as you reasonably can and thank them for their diligence.

Nonetheless, some reason-based restrictions on media access to a potentially hazardous scene are absolutely necessary. Three primary rules are reasonable and necessary for limiting the activities of reporters and photojournalists on-scene. Courteously but firmly and equitably enforcing them will help you maintain a reasonable degree of control of the scene while permitting the media representatives to obtain their story and images. The rules are:

1. *Media representatives cannot through their actions be permitted to endanger first responders or otherwise interfere with on-scene response.* A journalist who says or writes something that the police don't like has not violated the law. A media rep who physically endangers or otherwise interferes with the activities of first responders probably has. One common violation involves media camera operators lighting up a nighttime scene and, in the process,

endangering the SWAT personnel deploying there. That cannot be permitted. If you see such a careless act or something similar in progress or about to be perpetrated, it is your job to intervene immediately and forcefully. That does not mean that you start clapping people in irons. It *does* mean that you request that the dangerous action cease immediately and explain to the offending party why you are doing so. Most news people will get it and instantly obey your directions. In actuality they do not want to get your people hurt for the sake of some pictures.

2. *The media cannot through their actions be permitted to destroy evidence or otherwise alter a crime, accident, or incident scene.* Media types do not have any sort of special privilege that John Q. Public doesn't have that allows them to enter your protected scene. Crime scene barricades and tape apply to people carrying cameras and notepads, too. Media folks know this, but that doesn't mean that they will not push the envelope anyway in order to get a better picture or story than their competitor can glean. Your proper response is to courteously direct them outside of the area where they are not supposed to be with both an explanation and a warning. If the problem persists with the same individual, a stronger response may be advisable. In most instances that would involve a call to the offender's boss, either by you or your department's PIO. Follow your organization's guidelines for making a formal media complaint. But not unlike putting a media offender in handcuffs, it is always preferable to handle these issues on-scene without a more drastic response. It is also important to assure that the media misstep was not caused by a simple misunderstanding or unclear police instructions.

3. *Media representatives must not be allowed or assisted to break the law.* Journalists do not get a special pass allowing them to violate the law because they are accompanying law enforcement personnel on a scene. For example, a reporter or photojournalist who has attached himself to officers serving a search warrant on private property has no right to be there unless the property owner has granted permission. Once more, formal enforcement action should only be taken as a last resort. Experience has demonstrated that with virtually all journalists a simple caution to stay off of private property will suffice to accomplish your objective. The same rule applies in any other situation in which a media

rep feels the need to attempt to circumvent the law: politely (keep smiling!) notify him or her of the need to cease and desist, then observe to assure that your advice is followed.

Consider yet one more "prime directive" for working with the media on-scene while leaving everyone with their feelings intact: Unless you can voice a clear reason why a media rep should be forbidden from doing something, it is probably alright to allow him or her to proceed. Because you are an empathetic and ethical leader you may, for example, feel strongly that it is inappropriate to allow photojournalists to take pictures of a dead or mangled body on-scene. You have a good heart but realize that there is no law prohibiting such ghoulish behavior. No one has appointed you Chief of the Good Taste Police. As long as the picture-taker is in a place where he is legally allowed to be, you should permit him to continue with his actions. It is up to his boss, his readers, or his viewers to condemn his insensitive activities, not you. The days of a cop cupping his hand over a camera lens should be long past. Once again, however, you should very rarely encounter such conduct. Journalists have ethical standards, too.

A last word of caution: Anytime you are involved in or aware of a significant confrontation involving the media be sure you promptly notify your chain of command and your PIO (if you have one). Let them know the nature of the problem and what you did about it. You want these people to hear the story first from you, not from a disgruntled media person. With your good judgment and common sense in play you almost certainly handled it appropriately. Make the notification, don't sweat it, and move ahead.

Your responsibilities and duties on-scene are pretty easily summed up. Be readily accessible to the media. Remain calm and courteous. Provide the accurate information you can, realizing all the while that the media reps almost always will want more than you can or will give out. Enforce reasonable restrictions on the media's actions on-scene. Have a solid reason for all that you do. And, as always, through what you say and do serve as a terrific role model for your troops.

Finally, accept your on-scene interaction with the news media as yet another opportunity to excel. Maintain your usual, positive demeanor that has helped you be the successful leader that you are.

YOUR PERSONAL MEDIA GUIDELINES

You have a set of personal ethics and rules that serve well to guide you in your daily intercourse with others. They provide you with guidance in your professional as well as personal life. These same rules will help you in working smoothly and ethically with the men and women who represent the news media. Some of these guidelines are no more than extensions of good common sense. Others represent a reiteration of the tenets of the Golden Rule: Treat others as you wish to be treated in return. In addition to these trustworthy guideposts that you have long followed, you should find the following, personal media relations rules to be helpful when working with the press.

Always tell the truth. As a law enforcement officer your most precious possession is your integrity—your reputation for, among other things, telling the truth. A reputation for credibility is a must in working with the news media. Say nothing at all as opposed to stretching the truth. Lying by omission is still lying. The media representatives must know that what you say is the truth. If you lose your reputation for telling the truth to the media, you may never be able to recover it. You also will have seriously damaged your department if you are discovered in a lie to the press. As veteran CBS reporter Mike Wallace once said about police-media relations: "We will forgive you for not knowing. We won't forgive or forget if you are caught lying." Don't do it.

Don't hide from the media. Don't do it either figuratively or literally. Once the media reps know you are on-scene, trying to avoid contact will only result in aggravating them. Meet with each one who is seeking your attention. Experience has shown that once they have some information and perhaps some images many journalists will be ready to move on to the next story. The quicker you attend to their needs the more quickly you will get them out of your hair.

Don't allow yourself to be rushed. As you know, when you get in a big hurry you tend to miss things and make mistakes. You want to avoid that when working with the media. Even though you are likely to have a lot going on at the scene of a media "event" you will be doing yourself and the media reps a favor if you strive to avoid being rushed. You have not helped anything if in your rush you end up providing incorrect information or slip up elsewhere. When that happens, you will have to spend even more time repairing the error. Slow down and get it right the first time.

Know and follow your agency's media policies and procedures. Hopefully your department has provided you with written guidelines regarding what can and cannot be released to the news media. Being familiar with those guidelines will provide you with "official" backing for the decisions you have to make in responding to journalists' requests. Knowing the rules also will help you avoid making a critical error in how you handle the media and what you do or don't do.

Be patient, polite, and tactful. Even if the questions are really tough and the questioner rude and aggressive, you cannot afford to lose it and lash out, figuratively or otherwise. You cannot afford to surrender self-control and be less than courteous. If you do you will have lost both respect and trust, neither of which you can afford to discard when working with reporters. Staying calm and in control when dealing with the media will help you just as much as doing the same in the countless other stressful encounters you master. There will be times you have to say "no" to the media or deny them access to something or someplace. Do so courteously and always with an explanation of why. It is the treatment you would expect if the roles were reversed.

Keep your promises. Your word should be your bond in working with the news media. If you tell a correspondent that you cannot answer a certain question today but will tomorrow, be certain you make good on that pledge. If you say you will give an interview as soon as you finish your current task, be sure you do it. Again, your reputation for integrity and credibility is at stake.

Return calls and messages. It's possible that a reporter you met on-scene will have additional questions for you or request a follow-up update later. To maintain your reputation for credibility and dependability you should endeavor to return each phone call, e-mail, or text message as promptly as possible, considering that you have a lot of other responsibilities, too. Again, it's just the polite thing to do.

Use "off the record" judiciously. Once you have given a reporter a piece of information, he is under no legal obligation not to use it, no matter what he may have promised. Going "off the record" may be permissible if you know the reporter well and are convinced he or she will not print or broadcast what you have said on background or in confidence. But doing so is always a risk. Sometimes you may do it anyway to give a journalist a better picture of what is going on for the benefit of the agency, but be careful. The "safest" route is not to do it at all. Before you do be sure the potential gain is worth the risk.

Know that giving "exclusives" is dangerous. Giving a favored news media rep a desirable, "exclusive" piece of information that you have denied to his or her competitors is perhaps even more risky than going off the record. The lucky reporter may be at least temporarily in your debt but his competitors, who eventually will find out what you did, may be angry enough to file a complaint against you. Nothing says that you should not cooperate with a reporter was has found a good story or angle on his own. You certainly are not obliged to tell his competition what he is onto. But selecting him for special, privileged treatment or access is a bad idea.

Pick your media fights carefully. The misspelling or mispronunciation of your name is probably not worth a gripe to a reporter or his boss. You'd be well advised to let it go. Save your objections for errors of fact on the journalist's part. That's much more serious. Try to stay upbeat and nonconfrontational whenever remotely possible. If you come across as seemingly griping about everything pretty soon your complaining loses its effectiveness.

Don't hesitate to ask for help. Media outlets like to boast about the help they give to law enforcement. Believe it or not, most reporters and editors want to balance "negative" cop stories with good news about the men and women behind the badge. If you need the public's help in locating a bad guy or preventing a scam never hesitate to ask the media for publicity help. It is how they can repay you for taking care of them at a scene.

Trust where trust has been earned. There are really very few "bad" reporters, as there are very few rotten apple cops. There are lots of responsible, ethical journalists out there. Allow them to prove that to you over time. Once they do, it is perfectly fine to trust a bit. After all, that is what you are asking them to do for you. Some of them are even very likeable people!

Try to enjoy yourself. Media interruptions to the rest of your duties don't always feel pleasant. It will be best for your emotional health if you try really hard to take at least a little pleasure and pride in the fact that *somebody* wants to hear what you have to say. Maybe someone really important to you will even get to see you on the TV news, absolutely sparkling in the limelight! Or something like that.

Serving as Mr. Microphone is something you likely will have to do in your role as a law enforcement leader, at least occasionally. It just makes good mental health sense to enjoy it to the extent possible. Who knows, you might just get to like it.

Following these simple guidelines will make your job easier (and your life a little more stress-free) when you are working with the news media. They are really no more than rules for mature, professional behavior when you are relating to others, very possibly during an otherwise-stressful situation. Coupled with your extrovert's personality, they should serve you well no matter what the news of the moment.

DELIVERING A GREAT INTERVIEW

Your community's citizens will form much of their opinion of you and your department from what they see on television or the Internet, or perhaps hear over the AM/FM radio. A lot of this will result from the way you or another member of your department looks and sounds via the filter of the news media. That is why it is important that you do a good job when you are the one "on stage" at the moment.

You can do this, and do it well. You have the smarts, personality, and technical expertise to handle the challenge with ease. With the aid of a handful of "how to do an interview" tips you will take care of the journalist's needs at the same time you make yourself and your agency look great. Your interview may be for a newspaper or it may be recorded for broadcast on television, radio, or Internet news. It may even be broadcast or streamed "live." Most of the guidelines remain the same regardless of the medium the interview will utilize. However, the suggestions provided here have the video interview foremost in mind. If you can do a good job on the tube, it almost naturally follows that you'll do great via audio or in print, too. Those tips for giving a winning interview follow.

Ask the interviewer what he is after and what the questions will be. It is an absolutely legitimate question, and a professional journalist won't mind telling you. After all, he wants the piece to look professionally done, too. It will come across better if you have had time to research and plan what you want to say in response to his queries.

Gather the facts you will need. Go to the best source on-scene or elsewhere to get the answers to what you believe the interviewer's questions will be. Some of the answers you already may have from your own knowledge and observations. If you have not been able to learn the questions in advance, think "what would I want to know if I was asking the questions?" Then, gather the information needed to answer your own queries.

Double-check your information for accuracy. You are obliged to correct promptly any erroneous information that you find you have accidentally given to a newsperson. But there is a lot less work and embarrassment involved if you avoid giving out bad information in the first place. Be sure you have your facts straight before you answer a reporter's questions. Names and addresses, if to be released, absolutely must be correct. Do not give out details that are still hazy or unsubstantiated. Don't give out investigative keys or information forbidden for release by law. Instead let the reporter know that more details will be released later to the extent permitted by the statutes. You and the journalist have the same goal: get it right as opposed to lightspeed fast.

Anticipate surprise questions. Do not act shocked or outraged if during the interview a reporter asks you questions that he did not warn you of in advance. It is unlikely that he is playing dirty, although that is always possible. It is much more likely that what you have said has simply placed new questions in his mind. Or he may have thought of additional questions he hopes to have answered since he briefed you on what he planned to ask. Go ahead and answer what you can. Don't answer what you don't know. That's the correct (and safest) response.

Consider practicing your responses. You may or may not have time to practice your answers aloud before you do it for real. Doing it out loud may or may not be necessary. Many veteran interviewees go over their planned responses in their heads in the short time available before a planned interview, and that suffices to help them do a good job. You might want to plan the same routine. As you do more interviews the rehearsal you will need probably will decline to the point that you don't even require the silent, mental practice.

Check your appearance before a media interview. You are a working cop and it is OK to look like what you are. But it is advisable not to have pizza sauce on your lips, funk on your nose, or your hair going in 19 different directions before your starring interview appearance. Take a quick look, even if it's in a police car's rear view mirror, and straighten up a tad, if need be. You want to look like the professional you are and represent your department well.

Strive for a relaxed but professional appearance. There is a balance to be struck here. You don't want to project the image of a robot with a rod stuck up his backbone but neither do you want to look sloppy or slovenly. Your posture should be correct but not overly, falsely stiff. Keep your hands out of your pockets even if you don't think they are in view. The posture and attitude you might take for a conversation with a friend or colleague should work just fine. You are reaching for natural, not forced.

Avoid distractions as much as possible. Anything that would distract from the important things you have to say has no place on the interview scene. Turn off a squawking radio and silence your smartphone. Although real-life scenes can be naturally noisy, try to step away from the action as far as is acceptable to your interviewer. Unwanted noise is the enemy of every interviewer and interviewee. Avoid distracting mannerisms, such as "talking" extensively with your hands or chewing gum.

Maintain eye contact with your interviewer. Do what you would do in that fictional conversation with a friend or colleague: make and keep good eye contact. Do not look into the camera or permit your gaze to wander to something else. Stay focused on the person you are addressing.

Use a conversational voice in your interview. It is not necessary to raise your voice volume during an interview. Today's recording devices are quite sensitive. Once more, talk as you would to that friend or colleague in a normal conversation. And avoid slang or "cop talk" to the extent possible. The listener may not have a translator handy.

Keep your responses concise. A media outlet may use only a few seconds of your response. That is why it is vital to answer the question directly and in as few words as possible. This is not the place for war stories or lengthy explanations. If a reporter wants you to amplify on an answer, he will ask you to do that. Answer fully, but get to the salient points quickly.

Remain calm and in control. Even veteran speakers admit to a few butterflies before a speech or interview. A little nervousness can help keep you sharp. But the image you want to project is the calm and clearly in command professional that the listening or viewing audience immediately will trust and rely upon. As the old deodorant commercial goes, "never let them see you sweat."

If you can't or won't say, state that fact. There will be questions that you cannot or will not answer, either because you don't know or because the information is not something that should be released just now. The reporter likely knows that, but he is duty-bound to ask anyway. Let him know WHY you cannot answer: it's a personnel matter, it's an ongoing investigation, or whatever is the case. If you know that there is a time when the requested information will be available, let him know that, also.

Do not guess or exaggerate. If you know for a certainty that it really is the biggest drug bust in the state's history, it is alright to say so. But if you don't know that for sure, don't say it. It is absolutely necessary that what you put out to the media is factually correct, so guessing is out, too. This is not the time or place to make assumptions about what happened, either. Maybe it happened exactly that way in the last 12 incidents but didn't this time. Say only what you have confirmed to be factually accurate.

If you don't know, say so. You cannot know everything. The interviewer understands that. It won't make you look bad to say that you don't know, assuming you really don't. If you do know but cannot say for whatever reason, let your interviewer know that, too. But never, never say "no comment." There are too many more polite ways of saying essentially the same thing. The clipped "no comment" utterance will make you sound like a gangster in front of a U.S. Senate committee. Don't use it.

Treat all recording devices as eternally "on." More than one or two public officials have seen their careers go down in flames after uttering something they thought was clever at the time in the presence of a recording device they thought was "off." Number one, don't make those inappropriate comments in the first place. Second, assume that every recording device you see as well as those you don't is "live" and recording at all times, either intentionally or "accidentally." That rule applies to the time you spend with a reporter both before and after a planned interview. Make the assumption that you are being recorded as long as you are in the physical presence of an interviewer. Also assume that every media telephone call you take part in is recorded. There's a decent chance that your assumption is right on.

Watch out for the interview enemies. Most media interviewers, like most cops, are decent folks who are just trying to do a sometimes-difficult job well. But some are more talented or ethical than others. They might not be trying to trick you, they may simply be new on the job or not highly skilled at their trade. There are some interviewer approaches that, intentionally or unintentionally done, make it harder for you to get an accurate message out unless you overcome them. For instance:

Problem: The interviewer presents incorrect information in his statements or questions.

Response: Correct him (politely) immediately. You do not want to leave false information in front of the audience. Do this even if the interview is "live".

Problem: The interviewer repeatedly interrupts your responses.

Response: It may sound impolite but keep talking, over him if necessary. Again, you must see the correct information placed in front of the public.

Problem: The reporter asks you rapid fire questions without giving you sufficient time to answer the last one.

Response: It's an old defense counsel trick, right? He's hoping to fluster you to the point that you don't know which question you are answering. Just handle the interviewer the way you would the lawyer. Slow your responses and speak quietly. Ask him to repeat the question so that you are certain you understand it. Do not allow him to rush you. It is perfectly OK to do this even if it's a "live" interview. After a few rounds of this he may realize the futility of his approach and abandon it.

Problem: When you finish your answer, he stares at you expectantly without speaking.

Response: You may have used this one during a suspect interview. The hope is that the interviewee will fill the uncomfortable silence by talking some more, perhaps saying something he never intended to say. Refuse to play this game. When you have said all you intend to say, remain silent and stare right back. Again, after a volley or two of this he may desist.

Hopefully you will never encounter any of these interview shenanigans throughout your entire career. But now you'll be ready if you do. **Critique yourself to get even better for next time.** Watch yourself on video, if you have the opportunity. Do you see any mannerisms you don't like? Any nervous tics or expressions? How about voice and language? It's also alright to ask a friend or colleague who saw the show for an opinion on how you did. Do not overreact to minor issues.

Chances are you are your own harshest critic. Other folks may not have even noticed whatever it was that now displeases you. Just take note of what you want to do more or less of next time.

Chances are, you did a good job with your interview session. You don't have to be perfect or come across as an accomplished professional speaker. Viewers and listeners like to see interviewees as human beings like them, not perfect talking heads. As in many other activities of life, you get better at doing media interviews by doing them. Try to look at each one as an opportunity to showcase the very good things about your profession, your organization, and yourself. You have every reason to be proud of you and the good work you have done.

PREPARING A NEWS RELEASE

You are accustomed to preparing reports on crimes, incidents, and events. The purpose of these documents is, of course, to enable someone who wasn't there to see hear, feel, and perhaps even smell what occurred. It is likely that over time you have gotten pretty good at writing and/or reviewing these police reports of one kind or another.

A news release prepared for dissemination to the news media is just one more variety of report. It is, like the others, intended to inform those who probably were not present at the happening described. But its format is just a bit different from your "traditional" police report. It's shorter. It uses a bit different terminology. And the order and form in which its facts are presented differs from the offense or supplemental report you have long experienced. Its purpose is to allow a news reporter to prepare a story from the facts provided by the police. Many times, the release provides only the beginning of the story. It gives the journalist just enough information to begin his own investigation into what happened. He will then prepare his own summation of events for dissemination to the public as a news story on TV, radio, newspaper, or the Internet.

The news release is as important to your own organization as it is to the news reporter. It gives others in your agency a condensed version of a significant incident. It also notifies the rest of the world concerning what is going on in your jurisdiction and what your department is doing about it. Often it reports on good work done by your colleagues.

Anyone (including yourself) who can write a good police report can write an excellent news release, keeping in mind all the while that the two do have definite differences. There are some very useful guidelines that you can follow to prepare a news release that succeeds in effectively informing the media audience—and the greater public beyond. Those guidelines include the following:

Gather the information you will need. Just as you did for your interview assignment, seek out the sources of the information you will need to prepare the news release. Write down what you learn in order to help keep your facts straight. The information you will need includes what happened, where, when, and involving whom.

Carefully check for accuracy. Just like any other kind of police report, your news release must be accurate in what it states. Double-check for accuracy everything that is to go into the release. Your name is going onto the document so you want the contents to be correct. Both your own reputation for credibility and that of your department are at stake here.

Put a title on it. You should put a version of a "headline" on your news release, although it's unlikely that the media will use it on the finished product. The idea behind labelling your release is to let the news media representative or any other individual scanning it know what the topic is. The reader can then decide for himself if he wants to read further. That should tell you to make your "head" as informative and commanding as possible.

Answer the 5Ws and an H. Every good reporter knows what these are and that they belong in a news story. Every good police supervisor knows that they need to be in complete police reports, too. These are the who, what, when, where, why, and how of the incident you are summarizing for the press. Sometimes the answer may be implied and not something that you must answer. For example, why did the bad guy rob the bank? Most readers will assume without your telling them that it was to obtain the money inside. Keep the 5Ws and an H in mind as you are preparing your release. When it is done, check to see if you have adequately answered them in your written effort.

Use the inverted pyramid format. Picture a pyramid turned on its head. That's the style in which a journalist prepares his story. The most important facts go first and everything else follows in descending order of importance. That way if the story is cut by an editor due to a shortage of broadcast time or newspaper space the facts most likely to be of interest to a viewer or reader won't be left out. Prepare your news release the same way: most important facts first, everything else in descending order of importance. Try to get your 5Ws and an H within the first sentence or two.

Keep it to a page or less. Brevity is a blessing in a news release. Very lengthy ones often get tossed into the circular file without being read. If a reporter reviewing your concise account wants more details he will be in touch with you. Double-space your lines and be sure the type size is at least 12 point.

No opinions or editorializing allowed. A news release is not the place to write about "heroic officers" or "evil offenders." It's also not the place to comment on the guilt or innocence or character of any party. (Citing a confirmed criminal record is acceptable, of course.) Just report the facts and let the reader, listener, or viewer form his own opinions. Journalists are ethically bound to do the same, but occasionally a few of them forget that mandate. Don't join them.

Avoid "cop talk." Prepare your news release in the King's English. Omit the police jargon and legalese. "Perps" and "pinches" do not belong in your written product. Use the civilian and not the military version of reporting times and dates. In other words, it's 9 pm, not 2100. Fewer and fewer Americans have military experience. Don't force them to translate. Stay away from the acronyms and unfamiliar abbreviations, too. It probably is not helpful to write that the "operators from DART unit put out an ATL for a juvsexoff."

Proofread carefully for form and content. Read your release all the way through at least once to be sure you have covered all the pertinent details and that everything you have written is factually correct. Then read it at least once more to check for grammar or spelling errors. As you tell your rookies, in police work you are known by what you write and how you write it. Be certain that you get it right. A news release containing obvious errors can lose much of its credibility.

Provide authority and contact information. If a reporter is interested in your release he will want to contact you for additional details. By including your name and contact information at the close of the release you also give the information *authority,* something every reporter requires for his or her story. It allows him to attribute it to someone, who is now accountable for its accuracy.

Use all means available to you for dissemination. You should e-mail, text, and otherwise distribute your release to every news media organ in your area, even the ones who carry little local news. Your PIO should have a list of these organizations and their electronic addresses. That way you prevent any news organization from claiming that it got left out while potential competitors were "favored" by the cops. Some of the recipients will not be at all interested, but by distributing your release widely you appropriately place the decision to use your information or not on the media. The release also should be posted on all of your agency's social media accounts and website.

Be prepared for follow-up calls from the media. Realize that many reporters will use your news release as a "tip" or "lead" that requires additional work by them to flesh out the details. That will prompt them to contact you for more. Be sure that you return all calls and messages, even if there is little more you can add. In the process you build your reputation for credibility and reliability.

One of the best means for learning how to compose an effective news release is to copy what has gone before. It will help you to review past releases authored by members of your department. Beyond that, the following, fictional, sample release may provide assistance. This is a brief one, as many of yours may be, because it has been written early-on following a freshly-occurred incident. It may serve primarily as a "news tip" that tells reporters they will have more work to do a day or so later.

NEWS RELEASE
Smalltown Police Department

SMALLTOWN POLICE PROBING REPORTED HOMICIDE

Smalltown Police Department officers responding to a report of shots fired shortly after midnight Sunday, October 20 in the area of 1320 Elm Street discovered the body of a male adult lying in the driveway of that address. The man had suffered head trauma and was pronounced deceased at the scene by Justice of the Peace Melvin Smith. Officers arrested a male adult found inside the residence. He was tentatively identified as John Jones, age 25, of Baytown, Texas. He was placed in the Erath County jail pending the filing of murder charges.

The identity of the deceased man will not be released at this time pending the notification of next-of-kin.

The incident is being investigated by the Criminal Investigations unit of the Smalltown Police Department. It is anticipated that no additional information will be released until after noon on October 21.

Contact:

Sgt. George Hall
Smalltown Police Department
Telephone 303-970-1234
E-mail: george.hall@smalltownpd.com

This sample release covered a crime-related incident. Most of those you are asked to compose likely will be concerning criminal incidents or accidents. But you also could be asked to do a Public Service Announcement (PSA) describing a new scam for the public to watch out for or a publicity piece on departmental promotions or a new program being launched by the agency. The good news is that all are fairly similar in form. Again, the best guidance for you is to look at previous releases that have been written on these topics in the past. If you can create one kind of press release (and you can!) you certainly can do the others, too.

If you work at a larger department you might expect to prepare several news releases a year. If you labor at a small agency it may be rare for you to do one at all. Whatever your local situation you are now ready to handle the responsibility if it arises.

SUMMARY

As a leader of your organization you will be recognized as such by the reps of the media who spot you on the scene of a crime, accident, disaster, or some other newsworthy incident. In the absence of a police Public Information Officer or some other staff member willing to assume the responsibility you will be expected to attend to the needs of the media while keeping them from interfering with the work of the first responders on-scene. In the process you will be expected to make your organization and its people look good even as you reliably and accurately inform an information-hungry public via the media.

Like so many of the other responsibilities you handle on a daily basis you can master the challenges of being the Press Officer of the moment. It may surprise you to learn that some of your colleagues actually look forward to their interactions with the media and enjoy the opportunity to be a bit of a "ham." Hopefully you can learn to enjoy it, too. Whatever the case, you do not have to seek out the experience in order to do it well. You will give a great interview due to your friendly openness and your dedication to telling the truth and nothing but. You will construct an excellent news release because you are a good writer. You will work well with the media reps on-scene because you are a fair and accessible leader who enforces reasonable restrictions on their actions. All of these things in combination make you the kind of leader that a media representative is praying to find on an incident scene. You will be helped to succeed in all of these things because of the personal rules for working with the media that you have established for yourself. Foremost among them is your self-imposed mandate to always tell the truth.

Through your professional, considerate, and patient handling of the news media you can do a lot for your organization and your profession. Frankly, you likewise can benefit your own career within your agency. Every top leader is looking for personnel who can make the agency look and sound its best. By doing your usual, exceptional work with the media you will be among those personnel.

Chapter 16

SURVIVING YOUR ORGANIZATION

It is an admonishment you likely have given your officers more than once: it's not enough to survive the perils of the street. You also must be able to handle successfully the mental and emotional challenges of the job. It is sound advice and it is absolutely relevant for you, too. As a human being and a leader, you are exposed to the mental and emotional rigors of your difficult position every day. Some of those challenges to your mental and emotional good health originate within the walls of your own organization. How you respond to them will have everything to do with whether you have an enjoyable, successful career. Or something else.

Being a good leader brings stresses and pressures along with the insignia of rank. There are pressures from subordinates, superiors, family, and citizens. There are others that originate within you and your on-duty and off-duty life and personal needs and desires. Each is very real. Unless you are able to handle them successfully, they can lead to the undoing of both your career and your enjoyment of life and work.

Other people can help you. The support you hopefully enjoy from loved ones is one of your greatest assets. But you are the one primarily responsible for taking care of yourself. Just as you in your role as a professional constantly help others with their needs, so, too must you look out after your own physical and mental well-being. This chapter will offer you tips on how to best do that. Successfully navigating the political and organizational mine fields will aid you in surviving your own agency. Surviving the mines is a must for your career survival and ultimate job satisfaction. A list of some of those explosive devices is provided here. The idea is to steer clear of all of them but know how to survive and recover if you do clip one or more in your career-long journey. Finally, some suggestions are offered for staying "above the line" in all you say and do in your hopefully lengthy leadership career. It won't take you long to figure out that much of the advice is really no more than another version of the tenets of the Golden Rule that you learned as a youngster. It still works.

Your obligation to your family, your organization, and yourself is to assure that the job doesn't kill you. What follows is some help for reaching that worthwhile goal.

TAKING CARE OF YOURSELF

There is a reason that the flight attendant tells you to put on your own oxygen mask before you try to help anyone else. The fact is that you cannot help anybody until you first take care of yourself. That good advice applies as well to what you do as a leader. You will not be effective in aiding your internal and external customers unless you have seen to your own well-being.

There are a great many things you can do and refrain from doing to look out for your own welfare. For instance, in guarding your physical health you will be attentive of what and how much you eat and drink. By watching your diet carefully, you can avoid putting on the extra pounds that can set you up for a heart attack or stroke. By limiting your intake of alcohol, you can prevent excessive weight gain as well as under the influence behavior that can hurt others and damage or terminate a promising law enforcement career.

You already know that regular physical exercise is a must for someone who could end up defending himself from a criminal's attack or some other threat. You have a lot of choices for what you elect to do for exercise, but it needs to be consistent (preferably five days a week) and strenuous enough to get your heart rate up for at least half an hour. Check with your doc first, of course, if you have not been exercising for a while. In addition to helping take care of you physically, exercise can contribute to your mental and emotional good health by boosting your body's manufacture of endorphins, those internally-generated "feel good" chemicals.

Part of your prescription for good mental health also has to do with your attitude and perspective on life. Keeping a positive outlook to the extent feasible will take you a long way; so will letting go of the things that are beyond your ability to control. (You can hope and wish and pray, but you cannot really control whether or not the chief retires next year!) If you can master that art you will reduce greatly the number of things that actively worry you. As you know by now, excess worrying is not good for anyone's mental health.

But there's yet more you can do to stay healthy:

Don't have unreasonable expectations of yourself. You are not a superhero, nor are you superhuman. There is only so much you can do, only so many problems you can solve for others. You will be both physically and mentally healthier if you accept that reality. If you know that you have done all you reasonably can in solving any problem or navigating any situation, be content with that and try hard to let it go.

Ask for help when you need it. This is not necessarily advice to seek out a counselor or psychologist, but it could well pertain to that source of professional help, too. But there is plenty of other assistance out there. You may have to look no farther than a colleague in the next office or a really good friend. The point is that there are plenty of people in your world who are willing to lend you a hand (or an ear) if you just ask. Make use of that valuable resource. Then, return the favor anytime you have the opportunity.

Talk it out. Do not keep all of your fears, concerns, and troubles locked up inside. Have a confidant (or several) that you talk to about whatever is dominating your every thought. It doesn't have to result in a solution; just airing what's troubling you can have a cathartic effect. On the other hand, the conversation just might lead to a solution. It doesn't really matter who you talk with as long as you talk. A loved one will do nicely but so will a trusted colleague. Someone close but totally disconnected from your profession might be the best choice of all.

Realize that most crises have a short shelf life. It's true. Many things that are viewed as "nearly the end of the world" on Monday are largely forgotten by Friday. You may feel that a mistake you made today will be remembered and held against you for the rest of your life. That is highly unlikely. Bad tidings will pass. You can count on it because it's true. And speaking of that reality. . . .

One slip does not mean you are headed for Hell. No one is perfect. A lot of folks in your line of work fruitlessly try really hard to be. It's OK to make a mistake from time to time. Everyone does, generally on a daily basis. It's alright to forgive yourself for those occasional slipups. Chances are, everyone else already has.

Nurture your friendships outside of work. You likely will be physically and emotionally healthier if you have at least a few friends who are "normal" people. No one ever said that cops are normal. Those normal people also can help you hear the concerns and opinions of average human beings, not law enforcement professionals. Police people are sometimes accused of practicing "professional incest" in their thought processes. In other words, they form their opinions from talking to other cops. Having a few non-police associates may help you avoid those allegations, truthful or not.

Pick carefully the hills worth dying on. People in your line of work will always have professional differences on what at least seem at the time to be critically vital topics. In the final analysis, however, what color the chief decides to paint the police cars is probably not worth your threatened resignation if you disagree with his choice of palette. It simply doesn't merit nailing any of your key body parts to the wall, inasmuch as almost certainly the vehicles will still function as intended. Try really hard to keep things in perspective. Be certain it's worth a to-the-death brawl before you start the fight. Many things are simply not that important in the long run. If you determine after careful consideration that ethical or moral or legal principles demand that you take a no-holds-barred stand, then go for it by applying all your logic and powers of persuasion. Just be certain that whatever it is merits that degree of emotional energy output.

Don't do stupid. It may sound like crude or even cruel advice. But there's sound logic behind it. If you engage in unwise "extracurricular" conduct either on- or off-duty it is only natural that you are going to be worried about the fallout that results when your poor decision-making comes to light. Because you are the kind of person you are you may well spend a LOT of time worrying about that. Doing so will not exactly be good for your physical or mental health. The absolutely guaranteed solution? Don't do stupid in the first place. There are all kinds of stupid lurking out there. A police leader who drives after drinking would be seen as doing stupid. So would the married law enforcement leader who decides it's a good idea to chase badge bunnies. Don't do stupid.

NAVIGATING THE POLITICAL MINE FIELDS

For any public figure the landscape is liberally sown with figurative explosives that upon detonation could derail or terminate his or her career. The newscasts are full of stories of leaders, elected and otherwise, who suffer that sort of unceremonious fall. As a law enforcement leader, you qualify as a public figure. There also are plenty of smaller mines out there that, when detonated, may not draw attention from the media and the public but which will nevertheless result in serious or fatal career damage within your employing agency. Even if you survive their detonation you may find that your ability to lead and advance within your department is seriously compromised.

What are these career killers? Consider the following for starters:

Allowing your finances to become over-extended. Young cops are infamous for buying all the toys and spending every nickel they have–and then some. You may or may not still be a young cop, but not attending to your financial affairs in a responsible manner eventually will cause you plenty of trouble. Bosses don't like to hear from bill collectors or ex-spouses who are missing their child support. Be sure yours doesn't.

Participating in internal schemes, plots, and intrigues. If you have read much Medieval history you will recall that in those days it was not unusual for nobles and political opponents to engage in plots to kill the king and take power for themselves. Sometimes it worked. When it didn't, really, really bad things happened to the plotters. Enough said. Refuse to take part in conspiracies and power plays. Focus on doing your job instead.

Giving or receiving special favors and special deals. By virtue of your position you may find yourself faced with the opportunity to give or receive some thing or some deal not available to the regular Joe, perhaps including your subordinates. Look to your personal and professional ethics when such a temptation rears its head. As a law enforcement leader, you must do more than avoid wrongdoing. You also must avoid even the *appearance* of wrongdoing. Steer clear of "just for you" arrangements, whether you are on the giving or receiving end.

Being where you shouldn't be and doing what you shouldn't be doing. This no-no is relatively self-obvious as a career bomb. An example may be found with the police leader who finds it a good idea to be with a bunch of rowdy drunks in a bar at closing time. Or the police supervisor who hangs out at the boisterous after-watch party long past the time when the "bosses" were expected to leave. Use your good common sense on this one. It will keep you from having big regrets later.

Forgetting where you came from. Failing to remember where and how you started your policing career can bring you to grief if you forget the concerns of the people who are laboring in the trenches today. They are the reasons you have been appointed as a leader. Remember what your bosses did to irritate you when you were in those ground-level positions and try to avoid that kind of behavior. Remember what concerned you then. Similar things probably concern those ground-pounders now. Look out for them wherever and whenever you can.

Engaging in unethical or immoral conduct. As a leader you live your life, on-duty and off, in a glass house. The community wants to know that those appointed to enforce the law over them are following the rules themselves. Sexual matters interest virtually everyone, so if you are engaging in any sexual behavior that would result in public finger-pointing you are riding for a hard fall. What people may engage in themselves they often criticize in a leader. It's just the way the human animal seems to think. Cheating in any other way is also likely to bring you to grief once it sees the light of day. Remember: you are the positive role model everyone is watching.

Becoming complacent. You warn your officers against becoming complacent in their officer safety practices. You know that becoming complacent can result in their undoing, perhaps terminally so. Not paying attention to what is going on around you and in your own career can result in bad things happening for you, too. The fact that you are not hearing griping from your people does not necessarily mean that everything is rosy. They may simply have given up trying to reach you. Keep your head in the game. Law enforcement leadership is too dynamic an undertaking to successfully sleepwalk your way through it. Stay alert and involved every day.

Falling "below the line" in any respect. Sometimes leaders who have lost their way and begun to engage in questionable or outright bad behavior are said to have fallen "below the line." It means that they may have forsaken their ethics and bartered their integrity for the comfort or convenience of the moment. It can involve anything from cheating to outright criminal behavior. But it involves a general down-slide that if not arrested may destroy a career—your career.

There is a vaccination to prevent you from falling "below the line" and damaging or ending your leadership career through some of the self-destructive behavior noted previously. It calls for you to remain "ABOVE the line" in all of your actions. It requires that you remember who you are and what you represent. You are a leader. A law enforcement leader. That's something special, and it's something precious few can ever hope to be. Concentrate on what you want your legacy to be. Hopefully you will determine that you want to always be known as someone who did the right thing, most especially when the welfare of others was involved. It involves something called the Golden Rule.

THE GOLDEN RULE

It's really not that complicated. It is probably a component of your leader's personality in the first place. You treat others fairly. You remain "above the line" with them. You, in turn, expect to be treated fairly by those same people. It doesn't always work out that way, of course. Still, you persist in treating others in the manner in which you would *like* for them to treat you. It is nothing more complicated than the Golden Rule that you learned as a kid. It can amount to a win-win proposition for everyone.

But there is even more to it than that. There are some basic "people relations" guidelines that while basically following the teachings of the Golden Rule go just a bit farther in identifying a core of positive practices that when applied in your organization will help facilitate your efforts to experience a rewarding, contributing career even as you serve others. These personal guideposts for helping you relate to others and the organization as a whole include the following:

Never cease being a cop. Your subordinates will not expect you to be the best cop on the street, but they will expect to retain a cop's sense. Remember how to do the basics and do them right. When you stop to help one of your officers on the street (always the proper thing to do) he or she will expect that you still know how to provide cover, search a prisoner, or direct traffic.

Always do the right thing. Your officers are watching and most if not all of them want to be proud of their boss. Everyone else in the community is probably watching, too. That applies to your conduct on-duty and off. You need to be the world's greatest role model at all times.

Know how to listen. Whether they are your employees or your citizen-customers, sometimes they don't want you to fix something. They just want you to *listen* to what is on their mind. Granted, that can be hard to do for an action-oriented leader who wants to jump ahead to problem solution. But that may not be what they are looking for. Try hard to simply listen without interruption. Also, realize that it is not your job to fix everything that anyone ever complains about. At times you need to just listen.

Surprises are for Christmas—keep your boss informed. Most bosses are not too fond of surprises. Remember how you regard unheralded events that involve your own people. Keep your supervisor well-advised of significant happenings involving yourself and your employees. Err on the side of telling him or her too much as opposed to too little. Bosses do not consider that a problem. He or she will let you know if they want to hear less.

Never embarrass your boss through your own actions or omissions. This is a cardinal rule. If you do mess up, admit it promptly and let your boss know how you are going to repair the damage. Apologize if indicated, as it almost certainly will be. If you offer your supervisor explanation for the foul-up be certain that you do not include alibis or blame someone else. Own your mistakes as well as your successes. Your boss and your organization will expect that.

Respond to your mistakes wisely. Everyone makes mistakes. Oftentimes the mark of a leader is how he or she responds to the miscue. The formula for doing so is simple: Admit it. Fix it, if possible. Learn from the experience. Do not repeat it. Know that you can learn at least as much from your failures as you can from your triumphs. You will be OK.

Use humor often, anger seldom. No one likes to be around someone who appears angry all the time. Be able to laugh at yourself when that reaction is appropriate. Laugh at *appropriate* humor. If you are angry all the time the emotion loses its impact on others. Reserve your obvious anger for the very rare moments when you really must get your displeasure across to all in the vicinity. It will have a lot more impact that way.

Keep an upbeat attitude in front of your people and the public. In front of the public your people and your organization are always the best. Keep your critical comments to yourself or reveal them in the appropriate, private space. Your attitude is catching, and you want your people to be positive in their own outlook. Minimize the time you spend around really negative people. They, too, can be contagious. They may be infected with self-imposed misery that you do not need.

Be consistent. This is especially true in disciplinary matters. It also holds true for the standards you rely upon in evaluating the job performance of your people. Inconsistency will cause your subordinates to be uneasy if they have to figure out on a daily basis if they are dealing with Dorothy or the Wicked Witch. A good leader is positive yet realistic at all times.

Never show fear or uncertainty in front of your people or your boss. The people above you and below you in the police organization want to see you as the in-charge figure who has everything under control and knows what to do next. Even if you don't, rely on your acting skills to convince your audience that you've got it handled. You have done this more than once for citizens on-scene; do it for your own people, too. Self-confidence is catching, too.

Don't jump to conclusions. Don't make judgments before you have all the facts. Don't spout off before you know the whole story. Making baseless assumptions about what happened can bring you embarrassment when it turns out to have occurred in a whole different way. Wait until you are convinced you have all the relevant information you need to make an intelligent accounting.

Step back and take a look at yourself occasionally. Are your rank insignia getting heavy? Is your ego under control? Do you walk or swagger? Take the time to take an honest look at yourself and your behavior from time to time. Do you like what you see? Are you remembering to remain both ethical and humble in your interactions with others? Take a very honest look and act on what you see. There are plenty of people out there willing to help you remain humble if you miss the chance to do it yourself.

Show loyalty in all directions. You must display true loyalty to your subordinates, your boss, your organization, your profession, and your family. Speak up for all of them when necessary. Defend them when you must, but do not lie or cover up for anyone, ever. That's not loyalty. It's unethical and possibly criminal conduct.

Officer safety is always Priority One. Your subordinates doing the job of policing must know that their safety is always your utmost concern. Safety incudes their physical, emotional, and mental well-being. Whether it is needed training, equipment, or something else, your people must always know that you are looking out for their safety and survival. You have no more important task.

Remember that if you don't deal with the bad, you'll lose the good. OK, maybe they're not *bad,* but just a tad lazy or bored. The point is that your people know who's doing what they're supposed to be doing and who isn't. They don't want to be considered suckers for working hard while others slough off and receive equal pay and benefits. At some point *they* will start to slack off, too, if they don't see you dealing effectively with the malingerers. Those doing the job well have an absolute right to expect that of you. Don't let them down. Confront unacceptable behavior promptly and directly.

Always tell the truth. Your integrity and your credibility are priceless assets. Your subordinates and your superiors rightfully expect the truth and nothing but the truth from you, just as you expect it from them. Always uphold your end of the pact.

Don't dumb down your expectations if you meet resistance. Refuse to accept "good enough." Leaders do not lower their expectations if they meet resistance from one or more of their employees. Instead they work to bring others' standards up to their own. Sometimes that involves making plain the benefits that can accrue from exceptional performance to high standards. Stick by your guns and have the courage to demand excellence. Meanwhile, consistently deliver it yourself.

Remember there are two kinds of courage. You have the guts to lead your people in the search for a bad guy in a darkened building. You also must consistently display the courage to make the tough decisions, even when you know you will disappoint or even anger someone when you do. That calls for owning your decisions and not attempting to lay off the unpopular or less-than-successful ones on someone else.

Never stop learning your job. You want your people to get even better at their jobs. You must set a positive role model for them in always seeking to gather more knowledge, develop more skills yourself. On your last day at work you should still be learning more about what a leader is and should be. That is how both you and the profession get better.

One law for all. Do not do things or exercise privileges denied to your people. Obey the same rules they are expected to follow. If your people must qualify with their firearms quarterly, so must their supervisor. If your people cannot accept half-price meals, neither can you.

Rank may have its privileges, but cheating on the rules is not one of them.

Be a team player. It may sound both trite and corny, but it is what your boss expects of you. You must carry more than just your personal share of the load. A solid team can accomplish a lot more than a single, star player, no matter how talented he or she may be. In teamwork your interaction with your fellow team members will almost certainly help you in learning things and developing allies for the times when you need assistance.

Seek out a good mentor. There is a lot of knowledge and know-how stored in the senior staff of your organization. Tap into it by approaching a veteran leader and asking him or her to work with you as a mentor. Any real leader will be honored by your request. You probably will learn a lot. You also may have enlisted an important ally who will speak for you and your career interests in the future.

Don't start or pass rumors. You have got to talk with and listen to your people. That's important and it's what a good supervisor does. At the same time, you must do all you can to discourage the starting or passing of the rumors and ill-advised gossip that is to be found in every organization of human beings, yours included. Your organization's leadership expect you to curtail and prevent gossip, particularly that of the hateful, hurtful kind. It goes almost without saying that you are expected to refrain from instigating gossip yourself. Ask for the source when you hear a good tale. Chances are it will be hazy at best. Let your people know the damage gossip can cause and remind them that *they* could be the next victim of unfair rumormongering.

Save time for your family and yourself. It will help keep you balanced. Beyond that, it will help keep you sane. Do not try to become a workaholic. Little good will come from it. It's great that you have friends and support at work. That's important. But that should not substitute for the love and support you are hopefully receiving at home. It is doubtful that at the end of your life you will wish to have spent more time at work and less with your loved ones. If you are like most law enforcement officers, the support you have at home has enabled you to enjoy the career that you have experienced up to this point. Never forget that you owe a huge debt of gratitude to those who love you. Do not shortchange them.

Until and unless proven otherwise, assume you really can trust your boss and your organization. You may not always agree with the decisions made by those at the pinnacle of your organization. You would be unusual if you did. But, like you, the top leaders in almost all law enforcement organizations have good intentions and mean well. In the final analysis they are probably pretty decent people. It is okay to trust that they have the best interests of the organization's people at heart. If they really don't, they probably won't be at the top for long. Do them the favor of extending the benefit of the doubt. You would expect the same.

It would be easy to say that this formula for relating well to everyone else in your organization represents an unlikely if not impossible state of affairs for any real-world law enforcement organization in existence today. Perhaps that's true. But international disease prevention specialists have not given up on eradicating polio just because there are pockets of the malady still existing in some remote parts of the globe. They keep trying, keep working to wipe out a devastating disease. They don't surrender their ideal of a polio-free planet. They keep pursuing that incredibly important goal because it is worth doing for the worldwide benefit it would bring. It is, in other words, the right thing to do.

The same logic applies in your effort to help create a better, stronger law enforcement organization in which its members treat others in an "above the line" manner. Once again, it's the right thing to do. In the process of doing the right thing for the organization and its members you simultaneously will boost your chances for a successful leadership career as a part of that organization.

All of this *is* both desirable and absolutely feasible. Once more, you really *can* do it. Today is not too soon to begin the effort.

SUMMARY

You have chosen a difficult, demanding profession. Most people could not do what you do in the ethical and exceptional manner in which you do it. Accepting the burdens of leadership in that special profession has made the challenges to your physical, mental, and emotional health even greater.

But as you already have proven, you can do it. You do it by taking specific, common sense steps to help you avoid disaster in your physical or mental well-being. You do it by avoiding unwise, immoral, or just plain stupid behavior. You do it by taking care of others and, sometimes, letting them take care of you. You do not have to go your way alone.

Surviving your organization requires that you avoid all of the tiger traps that await the unwary. The career killers run the spectrum from the outright criminal act to the simply stupid. They include sexual picadilloes, complacency, enjoying special privileges denied others, and participating in backstairs plots, intrigues, and power plays. Your involvement in any of these things can bring a swift halt to a promising career. No matter how strong the temptation to participate, you must stay away from all of them.

The solution to avoiding being ensnared by any of these career-killing mistakes is to treat others within and without your organization in the same manner in which you would wish to be treated by them. It amounts to no more than the twenty-first century version of the Golden Rule. It requires that you check your moral compass from time to time and never surrender the ideals that brought you into a people-helping profession in the first place. None of this means that every single individual you treat well will reciprocate. But when you take the high road it will happen more often than not. It remains the right thing to do in life regardless of consequences or the lack of same. It is also the best way to survive and prosper in your own organization.

Remember always: stay above the line.

Chapter 17

PULLING IT ALL TOGETHER

The fact is that no matter what happens in the future, you already have served admirably in the cause of law enforcement leadership. You have applied your considerable knowledge, skills, and abilities in leading the incredible men and women who bring a human face and soul to a noble profession. You have trained them, guided them, and counseled them. You have done your best to see to their safety and welfare. You have listened to their concerns and done everything ethically and humanly possible to support them. You have been a very good supervisor.

You are by now in the process of pulling together all you have experienced and learned to continue to benefit your current team members and become even more skilled at helping the ones you will mentor in the future. You are assembling your own, personalized leadership handbook to accompany the one you hold in your hands. Together they will serve you well in leading the law enforcement employees of the twenty-first century.

As you prepare for the future you will take yet another look at ethics and how they apply to the leader's job. You will study your role as a member of your agency's leadership team. You will devise ways to get even better at what you do. And you will give careful consideration to what you want to do for the remainder of your leadership career.

Pulling all of these things together will help prepare you for the challenges you yet will face in a profession that produces new ones and new twists on old ones that show up virtually every day. Pulling them together requires yet one more look at the values and ethics that govern an exceptional leader like you.

THE ETHICS OF YOUR JOB

Your personal ethics require you to do the right things for the right reasons. That means you do them because you know that they are right, not because you fear that you might be caught and punished for doing them wrong. You also work in the light of the ancient-but-instructional Golden Rule as your directions for relating to others. You believe that it all starts with personal integrity, and you do your best to live your life and do your job that way. "Flavor of the month" pop management and the curious ethical guidelines it sometimes may foment are not your style.

Your ethics require that you utilize everything you have experienced and learned so far in life to benefit others, most especially the employees who depend upon you for guidance. In leading them you always strive to pull your people up to your own high expectations anytime that you find that their ethical standards are a little below your own. You never drop to a lower standard or expectation just because you have encountered resistance in what you are seeking to accomplish. Your goal is always to leave the place better than you found it when you arrived. That is what you want as your legacy.

It is understandable that as a law enforcement leader you focus on the ethics involved in supervising a team of employees. It is vital, however, that you additionally never neglect your ethical responsibilities to the community members you serve. Their rights, liberties, and freedoms must be respected and protected by the same government that can take some of those things away when an individual is duly and constitutionally found guilty of a serious crime. Those people, victims and offenders alike, deserve your ethical attention. By the excellent example you set you will once again serve as an exceptional role model for your employees who will be dealing with the same people. Ethics apply both internally and externally to the police organization.

You know well that you can keep learning more about ethics every day that you live. One of the things you already have learned is that what may initially feel easiest is often not what is ethically right. That in turn has taught you that sometimes it is important to challenge the "old way of doing things" when it doesn't pass muster with the cold realities of today's ethical challenges. Keeping that in mind you may find it useful to pose hypothetical ethical dilemmas to your peers and subordinates. What would be the *right* thing to do under those circumstances? Everyone has the opportunity to learn something from the discussion or debate that follows.

Yet again you will find yourself serving as an ethical role model for your charges. Your goal once more is to bring them to share your vision for ethics and ethical behavior. In the process of doing that you will help pull it all together for your subordinates, your agency, and yourself. You will have met another of your obligations as a good leader.

YOUR ROLE AS A MEMBER OF THE LEADERSHIP TEAM

You have skills and knowledge that they need. They have strengths and abilities that you require from them. "They," of course, are your fellow leaders and colleagues in the organization of which you are a member. You are all members of the same team. Your vision and goals for what the team seeks to accomplish should be the same, or very nearly so. The idea is that you will all work together to achieve those things. That is what the top leadership of the organization intends will happen. It is what your profession expects. It is what your citizen-customers—the taxpaying public—deserve.

You already understand that effective and efficient law enforcement requires teamwork. No matter how smart you are, no matter how good at your job you happen to be, you cannot do it well all by yourself. Yes, there may be times when you labor alone on a project or special assignment. You are certainly capable of doing that, and doing it competently. But there will almost certainly be more times when you must cooperate and collaborate with others to jointly accomplish important tasks. That is why your ability to work as an integral and contributing part of a larger group is so important.

Work is a component of teamwork. Being a contributing member of an effective team requires effort on your part. That effort requires that you volunteer your skills and abilities even before you are asked for help. It may turn out that you possess precisely the talent that is required to start or finish an important program or project. It is possible that your teammates won't realize that unless you come forward with your willingness to serve. It will be appreciated.

Being a good team player means that you shoulder your fair share of the workload. You surely can recall many of the work groups and committees you have been a part of all the way back to elementary school. You may remember how you felt when slackers in the group allowed others—probably including yourself—to do all or most of the hard work. Your law enforcement peers very likely will feel the same way if any member of the team fails to do his or her part. You do not want to be that team member. Even if the program or project your leadership team is tackling is not high on your list of favorite things be sure that you are a 100% participant in the group effort.

Get a little more comfortable with your fellow team members if you do not already know them well. Work to learn something about each of them. Let them know a bit about you, too. Any kind of joint effort tends to go more smoothly when you have a good working relationship with the people on your team. There almost certainly will be down time in whatever work your group is doing. Use some of it to get to know your teammates better.

One of the big benefits that can flow from a dedicated work group is that a whole lot more thinking and problem-solving may take place when several brains join forces as opposed to one thinking organ having to go it alone. Again: offer your help even before it is requested. Ask your colleagues for help when you are faced with a particularly knotty problem. You may be able to save yourself a lot of time otherwise spent rolling the issue around over and over again in your head. One or more of your teammates just might have the answer or solution that has so far eluded you. It is always worth a try.

Equally important is the demeanor you maintain while working with your teammates. Always openly put forward your views and opinions during problem-solving discussions and debates. Advocate for your beliefs and never be afraid to speak up, even if it feels at the time like you are the Lone Ranger in the stand you have taken on a given topic. There is danger in groupthink and you don't want to change your stand just because you were pressured and stampeded by other members of the team. Always feel free to disagree, just be respectful of others' views when you do. At the same time, be open to changing your mind when you are presented with sound, logical arguments and facts. Even extreme differences of opinion can remain civil when everyone agrees to remain above the line. This is not the time or place for personal attacks or the airing of old grievances.

When the discussion is done and a consensus decision reached it is most often desirable that each team member supports the group's position. Argue as vehemently as you feel you must while the debate is underway. Remain courteous to others in doing so, of course. But once the group has made its decision do not be guilty of sniping or otherwise criticizing the final outcome. Even if the group's decision or action turns out later to be less-than-perfect or even outright bad, resist the very strong (and very human) temptation to criticize and disclaim the group's work. Attacking your fellow team members is a great way to lose friends and make enemies. You do not need to do either.

Finally, remain humble concerning your role in the group's work and ultimate work product. Be quick to give credit to your team members. It is alright to play down your own role. Your colleagues know of your contributions. It's important that others hear from you that it was the team that deserves the credit. That's being a team player of the first magnitude.

HOW CAN YOU GET EVEN BETTER?

Doubtlessly your personal ethical beliefs require that you work continuously to get better at this job called leadership. You realize that your ethical obligation is to never cease learning. It also makes sense to step back and do an honest self-assessment from time to time. Be frank with yourself. What do you feel you are doing well and where might you need some work? How can you strengthen your leadership skills? Vow to fix it when you discover a knowledge or skills gap.

You can expand your awareness of how you are doing by having at least one more set of eyes look at your work. Ask your boss for his or her opinions. It is likely that your organization has some sort of performance review program in place. Certainly, you can learn from what your supervisor has to say there. But sometimes job reviews done at the managerial level are somewhat formulaic and contain a limited amount of truly useful information. (That would not happen with a performance review that you authored!) Learn what you can from the document and the annual sit-down with your boss that likely accompanies it. Then, ask him or her for some personal, in-depth opinions on how you are doing. If the boss does not already know your career plans and hopes, this is a good time to lay them out. Ask for suggestions on what else you could do in order to get there. You do not necessarily have to accept everything your supervisor says as the gospel. But all of it is worth your careful consideration. You will learn *something* useful to help you get better.

There is more you can do in your meeting with your supervisor. Let him know that you want to learn more of his job. Volunteer to help with whatever projects or other tasks he has on his plate. There may be something that he just doesn't want to handle that could be done by someone else. Someone like you. You will learn things by carrying out such tasks under your supervisor's direction. That will be knowledge that can help you in the future. You are also very likely to receive your boss's appreciation for your selfless work. *That* is something that is good for your future, also.

While you are in the volunteering mode, volunteer for relevant training that will boost your job knowledge and reinforce your career plans. You can never know too much. Even if you are required to invest some of your own funds in getting as much leadership training under your belt as possible it should prove useful down the road. Take advantage of every opportunity at further education.

There is something else you can do that will help others at the same time you help yourself. Consider mentoring and coaching a leadership trainee. Offer your assistance to an interested and upwardly mobile subordinate. The experience will benefit you as much as it does the trainee. Being in a teaching mode will help keep you sharp as you think about the leadership lessons you will discuss with your trainee. You will be better for the effort on top of the self-satisfaction you will enjoy in helping construct your profession's future.

But your trainee is not the only one who can learn from what others are saying and doing. You can pick up a lot from your observations of other leaders, including some that are outside of your profession. As you know by now, oftentimes you can learn more from the mistakes and failures of others as you can from their successes. Keep up with current events at the local, state, and national levels. The news stories never lack for tales of leaders falling from grace. Most often enough details are provided to inform you of how it happened. You can learn what *not* to do or say from each of these stories. Keep learning from your own little stumbles, too. They hopefully will be few in number but each holds a nugget of knowledge just waiting for you to mine it.

Do more than look at the mistakes of other leaders, within and outside of your field. Pay attention to those you have reason to respect and admire. What is it about them that you like? Is it their demonstrated technical knowledge or people skills? Most probably it is the latter. Or it could be both. Whatever the case, whether the individual you admire is on the local or national stage, keep an eye on the tactics and techniques they utilize when working with others to reach a goal, whatever that target may be. You can glean knowledge from his or her triumphs and disasters. How the individual responds to the disasters can be especially helpful to you in your quest to become a better leader. Failure can be a great teacher.

As you continue to work at getting even better as a leader your exposure to other leaders and their ideas sometimes may cause you to question some of your own, perhaps long-held beliefs. That's perfectly normal for a leader like you. Be willing to change your views and opinions if you discover solid evidence that something you have long believed is actually questionable or outright invalid. Part of being an intelligent, mature leader is knowing when it is time to change. Because of who you are you are always learning. That's good. Life-long learners are always bolstering their knowledge accounts and sometimes changing their views in response to new experiences and knowledge. You are certainly capable of doing that.

At one time or another you probably have encouraged your subordinates to play mind games with themselves. That is, you have encouraged them to run hypothetical crises and other situations through their minds and develop potential responses should they face an identical or similar situation for real one day. The same sort of mental game playing can work well for you in your quest to become an even better leader. Run some of those leadership challenge scenarios through your mind. What would you do when faced with one or more of them? Develop some response options. Be prepared to modify them as you give the scenarios more thought. There is evidence that officers who have thought through officer survival challenges in advance do better at safely resolving them when they erupt for real. The same thing can work for you when the tough calls are of the leadership variety.

Pulling it all together requires that you never stop working to get better at what you do. What you do is lead. Always keep pursuing your goal of personal leadership excellence.

WHAT'S NEXT?

Are you happy where you are? If you are comfortable and satisfied in your role as, say, a Patrol sergeant and eventually want to end your career in that position, go for it. There is not a law enforcement organization in America that has enough talented Patrol supervisors. If you do want to do something else, what is it? The next question you should ask: Is your goal realistically within your reach? Neither over-estimate nor underestimate what is potentially within your grasp. If you are a first-line leader with a GED in a six-officer department in a small West Texas town becoming chief of the Los Angeles Police Department is probably not realistically within your reach. But becoming chief in your own agency or a somewhat larger one certainly is. Now is not too early for you to begin your journey in earnest to reach the slot you would like to fill one day.

Are you so comfortable in your organization that you would not consider going to another one for career advancement? Are family or other concerns going to keep you rooted in your current community or are you willing to relocate if the right opportunity beckons? Just how mobile are you willing to be in your career planning? Many cops like structure and the familiar because of the uncertainties their job throws at them every day. How important are those things to you? If you feel you will be seriously traumatized by a major move outside your comfort zone then that sort of career move may not be right for you. Time constraints also may play a role in your career planning. How far along are you in your law enforcement career? Your options for starting over may be fewer if you are well along in your career as opposed to just starting out.

Do an honest assessment of your strengths and challenges. Keep building on the strengths you identify. It is impossible to be too good at what you do. Where you detect challenges develop action plans to deal with them successfully.

There are yet more questions to be answered. What education and specialized training will be required to achieve your career plans? Find out what you need and make a plan to get it. What other bases need touched? Missing one now could delay or even prevent you from reaching your desired target. Some leaders have been known to keep a list and check off the career accomplishments as they accumulate.

Now is the moment to starting making preparations to get where you want to go. Among those preparations is making sure that your loved ones on the home front share your goals and will support you in your drive to get there. They need to know that they, too, may have to make sacrifices in order to help you get there. Succeeding without that key assistance will be difficult for you if not impossible. Some honest discussions are in order.

You also will want to identify others who may be able to help you with your career plans. A solid mentor can assist a lot. Let your immediate supervisor know what you hope to accomplish one day. He or she almost certainly will be willing to help if you just ask. It is often a good idea to ask your agency's top leaders for their opinions and advice for your career planning. First of all, you likely will gain useful information. Secondly, they will be flattered that you feel they have something to offer. They may resolve to assist you in the future as you continue your upward climb.

Be sure that you are doing *something* to help you reach your career goals at every opportunity. Every opportunity translates to every day. Forward movement should be continuous. If you are not advancing you are, at best, standing still. That is not how to gain the future you seek.

Realize that doing an exceptional job in your present position is the most reliable means for assuring that you one day will have a good shot at something else. Like you, the Big Bosses do not promote someone or award them a special assignment because they are loafing or floundering in their current job. Be sure that you always do your best at whatever the task of the moment. It is bound to be noticed and that is a big plus for your future plans.

Dare to dream and plan big, but remain flexible in your planning. An opportunity may show up that you had not even considered. One municipal police mid-manager who had his eye on an assistant chief position in a neighboring jurisdiction was surprised when the same job suddenly became available in his own department. He competed and won the prize. The lesson: stay alert and open to *all* possibilities. Be willing to alter your plans if it makes sense to do so. Give it careful thought before making your move. But know that changing directions is a perfectly acceptable decision once you have thought it over and considered all of the ramifications.

A word of caution, however. Do not make critical decisions concerning your career plans immediately following serious trauma or during moments of strong emotion. You may be boiling mad at your organization and its bosses today, but this is not the time to quit and go to work at a drastic cut in pay for Tinytown Police Department. Give yourself plenty of time to calm down and think. As you consider all of the repercussions of leaving angry and starting a whole new career the idea may begin to look less attractive. Even if you ultimately reach the same decision, leave yourself time for rational consideration. Think—a lot—before you act rashly.

Perhaps your plans include running a law enforcement agency of your own one day. If that is your goal, it is especially important that you begin preparations in earnest right now. Get the formal education leadership training you will need, even if you have to pay for much of it yourself. Most chiefs' jobs now require at least a four-year college degree. Graduation from a top law enforcement leadership school such as the FBI National Academy or the Senior Management Institute for Police run by the Police Executive Research Forum will be extremely helpful if your agency will spring for sending you at some point. Again, let your bosses know of your future plans. They may be willing to help you. Making the acquaintance of the leaders of some executive search firms can help, too, as will keeping track of CEO job openings advertised on-line and in law enforcement's professional publications. That will give you a feel for position requirements and job descriptions. Meanwhile, strengthen your resume at every opportunity.

As you plan for what comes next in life you may find that the next logical step lies outside the familiar confines of law enforcement. That's alright, too. Your in-depth experience as a law enforcement leader may have qualified you for positions in the private sector that may be more lucrative than remaining in your current uniform. Depending upon your educational background, teaching or consulting may be possible options for you. Shed any blinders that may limit your field of vision to only what you have done in the past. You also should be looking at what you want to do well past the end of your law enforcement career. People are living longer these days. If you want or need to continue working a while longer your leadership background probably has prepared you for some other jobs. Take a good look at what is out there and make connections. The popular term these days is *networking*. Whatever you call it, making plenty of contacts in the worlds beyond policing just makes good sense.

No matter how much planning you do, it's important to remember that life often throws wrenches into the machinery of the best planning efforts. All kinds of accidents and incidents can befall even the best planner. A serious injury or illness may temporarily sidetrack you. There may be personal issues of a distracting nature at home, such as a separation or divorce. Financial troubles may rear their ugly heads. You may be the recipient of significant discipline for something you did in a moment of poor judgment. All of these planning obstacles are real, but most all of them can be overcome. Your career progress may be slowed for a time, but that does not mean that it has to stop. Just keep working at it. One well-known police chief once confessed that he had probably been disciplined more times than anyone else in his old department. But each time he apologized for his mistake, fixed it as best he could, and learned from the experience. He went on to be a successful police chief. It is likely that, with sufficient effort, you can make a similar recovery from a temporary setback.

Most law enforcement leaders did not succeed in achieving their goals the first time they tried for them. Be prepared for those occasional failures and frustrations. Another successful chief recalled that he had endured more interview processes than he could remember before he finally landed a desired post. You may get exactly what you are seeking your very first time out, whether it is a special assignment, promotion, or a whole new career. But most of your colleagues don't. Keep at it and don't lose hope.

Determining what's next for you requires that you determine what it is that you want to be doing in both the immediate and distant future. It mandates that you plan your next moves from where you are right now while you keep doing an exceptional job in your current assignment. But do not neglect that more distant look down the road, perhaps into your next career, true retirement, or both. It is not too soon to begin that journey today.

SUMMARY

In the final analysis it turns out that the law enforcement employees of the twenty-first century are not greatly unlike their predecessors from the previous century. It is true that they have a few additional skills. But it is also true that some may need to polish up on a few things that their predecessors did better. They have their own ideas of how they should strike a favorable work-life balance. They like to communicate a bit differently than did the police practitioners who went before them. And many of these good people look at their employer's rules and rule-enforcers somewhat differently than you did as a new cop.

But with all the differences these twenty-first century cops were most often attracted to law enforcement for the same reasons that you were. They want to help other people. They believe in justice. Some of them don't mind an occasional adrenaline rush. They want stable employment and don't want to worry about getting a pink slip the next time the Stock Market takes a tumble. They probably decided on law enforcement as a career for some of the same reasons that you did.

Overall, the quality of the people entering policing today remains high. Some have little life experience. For many their book smarts outweigh their street savvy. Many may not have experienced the hardships that you did before and after taking the job. But most remain good people who perhaps more than ever need a wise and firm leader to guide them. That leader must be you.

In this book you have learned to assemble your box of leadership tools and form a good working relationship with your crew. You have learned how to work well with your own supervisor and make the really tough decisions, tactical and otherwise. You have strengthened your abilities to work as a trainer, report reviewer, performance appraiser, and safety officer. You have picked up useful tips on counseling and disciplining employees—including the really "difficult" ones. You have gained additional skills for handling unhappy citizens and persistent members of the news media. You have picked up additional tools for leading your people to provide exceptional service. Finally, you have received some important and experience-proven advice for surviving the politics and other peculiarities of your own organization. All of these things that you have done will serve to make you an even better leader in the future.

As a leader you are a problem-solver. This is your problem-solver's manual. Keep adding your own chapters as you continue to learn and prosper in the noble profession of law enforcement.

INDEX

A

Abilities, 66
Absences, 109
"Above the line," 185, 191
Absolutes, 40
Accidents, 95
Acclaim, 72
Accountability, 22
Accuracy, 84, 169
Action plan, 47
Agreement, 114
Alcohol abuse, 108–109
Anger, 186
Apathy, 92
Apology, 148
Appeal, 125
Appearance, 169
Approach, 42, 93–94
Assess, 46
Assistance, 47
Assumptions, 92
Attitude, 97, 186–187

B

Backup, 93
Behavior, 112
Behavior, disruptive, 131
"Below the line," 184
Bias, 35, 79–80
Body language, 143
Boss, 21, 25–26, 33, 87, 190
Bullying, 131

C

Career killers, 183–184
Carelessness, 92
Challenges, 130
Change, 138
Citizen-customer, 144
Colleagues, 122
Command, 46
Command presence, 11
Common sense, 7, 38
Communication, 6, 19, 39, 67–68
Comparative discipline, 123
Compassion, 50
Competency, 6
Complacency, 92
Complacent, 184
Complaint, 108, 142, 146
Concerns, 110
Conclusions, 187
Conduct, immoral, 184
Conduct, unethical, 184
Confidant, 106, 117
Consensus, 195–196
Consequences, 39, 123
Control, 47
Conversation, 112
"Cop talk," 175
Counselee, 114
Counselor, 106, 117
Courage, 9–10, 16, 38, 49, 83, 188
Cover, 94, 99
Credibility, 161
Crew, 130

Crises, 181
Critique, 172
Curriculum, 59
Customer service, 151–152, 156, 157–158

D

Danger, 92
Danger signs, 100
Debriefing, 54
Decision, 37, 44, 195–196, 203
Decision-making, 34–35, 43–44, 45
Demeanor, 108
Demobilization, 48
Deployment, 51
Details, 79
Directions, 47
Disagreement, 86
Disciplinarian, 119, 128
Discipline, 119, 126
Distractions, 52, 112, 170
Documentation, 17, 85, 124
Drug abuse, 108–109

E

Editorializing, 175
Ego, 41
Emotional involvement, 35
Emotional outbursts, 109
Emotions, 113, 124, 136

Empathy, 38, 50, 90, 145
Employee, 5, 129
Employee Assistance Programs, 116
Ethics, 193
Evaluation, 61–62, 87
Evidence, 36, 82
Exception, 23
"Exclusives," 167
Exercise, 180
Expectations, 8, 15, 124, 181, 188
Experience, 36, 42, 95, 203
Eye contact, 112, 170

F

Facts, 111
False courage, 93

Family, 189
Fatal errors, 96
Favors, 183
Fear, 32, 187
Field Training Officer, 56
Finances, 183
Fitness, 100
Flexibility, 50
Follow-up, 88, 125, 137, 176
Friendships, 182

G

Goal, 6, 60, 83, 138, 202
Golden Rule, 165, 185
Grammar, 70
Grooming, 110
Guidelines, 165

H

Handcuffing, 94, 100
Hands, 101
"Headline," 174
Help, 49, 71, 99, 137, 181
Hero, 98
Hesitancy, 36
History, 36
Hot buttons, 144
Hot reactor, 25
Humor, 186
Hygiene, 110

I

Ideas, 43
Incompetent, 26
Information, 37
Innovation, 64
Insubordinate, 131
Insubordination, 21–22, 109
Integrity, 16, 161
Intelligence, 38
Internet, 168
Interview, 168, 171–172
Interviewer, 168
Intrigues, 183
Inverted pyramid, 174–175

J

Journalists,163
Judgment, 38

K

Knowledge, 37, 49, 53, 66

L

Language, 70
Leader, 12, 74, 103, 118, 128, 149
Leadership, 55, 139, 198
Learning, 53
Legal advisor, 135
Lesson plan, 60–61
Lone Ranger, 195
Loyalty, 6, 15–16, 187

M

Mentor, 189
Mindset, 98
Mine fields, 183
Miscommunication, 150
Mission, 19, 83–84
Mistake, 8, 122, 186
Misunderstanding, 150
Modesty, 50
Morale, 8

N

National Academy, 201
Negative discipline, 120
Networking, 201
News media, 159–160, 176
News release, 173–174
Noise, 35
Notes, 88–89

O

Objectives, 60
Officer safety, 91, 97, 104, 187–188
Officer survival, 102
"Off the record," 166

Opinions, 175
Opposition, 79
Options, 114
Organization, 179, 190
Outline, 61
Overview, 60
Ownership, 49

P

Patience, 49–50
Peer support programs, 116
People, 48
Performance appraisals, 75
Performance review, 77, 80, 89–90
"Personality conflict," 134
Perspective, 41
PIO, 163
Plan, 51
Planning, 202
Plots, 183
Police Executive Research Forum, 201
Police psychologists, 116
Politician, 26
Positive discipline, 119
Post Traumatic Stress Disorder, 48
Praise, 19–20
Prejudice, 35
Press Officer, 178
Preview, 85
Principles, 49–50
Prisoner handling, 95
Problem, 87, 107
"Problem employee," 129
Problem-solving, 49–50, 111
Procrastinating, 78, 122
Procrastination, 35
Profession, 190
Professionalism, 161
Professional Standards, 147
Progressive discipline, 123
Proof, 23
Proofreading, 70, 175
Protective equipment, 94
Psychology, 5
Public Information Officer, 162, 177
Public Service Announcement, 177

R

Radio, 168
"Reactionary gap," 99
Reasonableness, 162
Reassurance, 154
Recovery, 202
Relationship, 30
Relaxing, 95
Reliability, 7, 154
Report, 4, 71, 73
Report-writing, 67–68
Research, 133
Resources, 115
Respect, 154
Responsibilities, 22–23
Responsiveness, 154
Review, 82
Risk management, 91, 104
Risks, 49
Role model, 7–8, 102
Rumors, 189
Rushing, 35

S

Safety, 103
Safety practices, 101
Schemes, 183
Searching, 94, 100
Self-confidence, 4
Self-critique, 42
Self-discipline, 119
Self-doubt, 32
Senior Management Institute for Police, 201
Setback, 202
Share, 47
Shortcuts, 83
Skills, 58, 66
Solution, 114
Sources, 61
Spelling, 70
Standards, 6
Status quo, 36
Stupid, 182

Subordinates, 14
Success, 117
Summary, 87
Supervisor, 27, 127
Surprises, 22, 31, 82

T

Tactical, 52–53
Tactical decisions, 54
Talk, 113, 181
Tardiness, 109
Team, 13, 18–19
Team player, 189
Teamwork, 194
Television, 168
Threat, 94, 101
Timeliness, 39
Tombstone Courage, 9, 97
Toolbox, 3, 12
Trainer, 56–57, 66
Training, 38, 65
Traps, 78
Triage, 50
Trust, 16, 167
Truth, 22, 83, 188
Truthfulness, 16
Twenty-First Century, 202

U

Uncertainty, 187
Understanding, 90
Use of force, 109

V

Veteran, 24
Vision, 7
Volunteering, 23, 197

W

Wallace, Mike, 165
Weapon retention, 94